Martyrs of Magadan

Memories of the Gulag

Martyrs of Magadan
Memories from the Gulag
© 2007 **Aid to the Church in Need**

Testaments collated by Fr Michael Shields
Text edited by John Newton and Terry Murphy
Design by Terry Murphy
Photographs courtesy of Patrick Delapierre/Church of the Nativity of Christ, Magadan, Russia and the private collections of survivors of the camps.

Published by
Aid to the Church in Need (UK)
12-14 Benhill Avenue
Sutton
SM1 4DA
Tel: 020 8642 8668   Email: acn@acnuk.org
Fax: 020 8661 6293   Website: www.acnuk.org
Registered with the Charity Commission No. 1097984

ISBN 978-0-9553339-4-1

Front cover photo: The 'Mask of Sorrows' in Magadan, erected in memory of the 'repressed'.

Back cover photo: The convict number painted on Bronislava Klimavichute's shirt during her time in the gulag. The number is on display in the Church of the Nativity, Magadan, as a permanent reminder of the camps.

"People died by the tens, hundreds and thousands. In their place always came new silent slaves, who laboured for some food, a piece of bread.

"They died and they were quietly buried. No one had a burial service for them, no family or friends paid their last respects. They did not even dig graves for them, but rather dug a communal trench. And they tossed the naked bodies in the snow and when spring came, wild animals tore apart their bones.

"We who managed to survive mourned them. We believe that the Lord accepted these martyrs into the heavenly kingdom.

"May all these peoples' memory live on forever."

Olga Alexseievna Gureeva
Prisoner in the gulag camps for 11 years

В безымянных
могилах
Мы закончили век.
Кто забыть о нас в силах,
Если он человек...

"In this unmarked grave our lives have ended.
Who could forget about us if he is a human being?"

Contents

Martyrs of Magadan:

Foreword by Neville Kyrke-Smith

FAITH HELPS PEOPLE ENDURE SUFFERING. In Soviet times, Stalin's communist regime sought to drive God's spirit out of a faithful people – to create a frozen spiritual wasteland in Siberia to mirror the cruel, harsh terrain where the gulag prison camps were established.

Hundreds of thousands of innocent people were seized – from their homes, their villages, even their churches. They were subjected to torture, beatings and interrogation, before being banished to forced-labour camps, often without trial. Their alleged crime? They were enemies of the state – an atheistic and totalitarian regime.

The true extent of what took place in the Soviet labour camps has long been veiled from the world's eyes. The authorities were determined that the world should never know the stories of suffering and inhumanity; and the silence of collusion has made the stories hard for Russians to tell. For those who survived, recalling their horrifying experiences was too distressing to contemplate.

Now we can read their stories. **Martyrs of Magadan** is a testimony of faith in the face of brutal, inhuman treatment. That these people could live through the frozen hell of the Kolyma prison camp and still cling to their faith is a miracle.

Historically, Russia has been a crucial area of the work of Aid to the Church in Need. Father Werenfried van Straaten, the charity's founder, saw the desperate need of a faithful forced to endure cruel communist oppression, and he himself took great risks to work to preserve the Faith behind the Iron Curtain. Today Aid to the Church in Need supports Catholic, Russian Orthodox and ecumenical projects in Russia, in response to Pope John Paul II's exhortation that to help our Orthodox brethren is "an imperative of charity".

The rebirth of the Faith in Russia would have been unthinkable without the courage, endurance and unswerving faith of hundreds of thousands of these survivors of persecution. Let us pray that their example may be an inspiration to us all.

Neville Kyrke-Smith
National Director
Aid to the Church in Need UK

Introduction by Father Michael Shields

IT HAPPENED AT THE END OF the 1990s, after the 8 o'clock Saturday morning Mass, which was offered every week for those who had suffered and died in the former prison camps of Stalin in the Kolyma, in the far-flung east of Russia. Olga from Ukraine and Bronislava from Lithuania, two Catholic women who by some miracle survived the inhuman treatment and conditions of these infamous camps, were to give their testimony at the Marian Congress in Irkutsk. Both of them had been arrested in their early twenties because they believed in God, which made them "enemies of the people".

I stayed behind in the chapel with Marie Javora, the head of the Madonna House community, to listen to the testimony of Olga. She wanted to rehearse her talk. It would be the first time she would publicly witness to the brutality of her 20 years in the prison camps. The words were so simple and direct that they hid in their simplicity a depth of pain that is beyond imagining.

As she began, her voice quivered. Then pausing and holding back her tears, she quietly said: "It is so painful to remember." I felt as if a sword went into my own heart, and for one split second, I seemed to be sharing in her pain. She continued: "Only those who lived through it can really know what it was like. The hunger, the freezing cold, exhausting labour, a regime beyond our strength, the taking away of privileges... It was only God who saved us. Never once did I doubt him. I never cried or blamed him for what had happened to me. Faith never left me. It was prayer alone that strengthened my soul and body."

I have lost count of how many times I have heard that painful cry from the heart of the camp survivors: "It is so painful to remember." But we must remember that these women and men are living examples of Christian faith and of how prayer strengthens the heart to bear the harshest realities, even the cold suffering of the Siberian prison camps.

How many died in the camps in Russia is unknown. They died while being tortured in the interrogation prisons before they could be sent on elsewhere, deported in railway cars. They died packed like animals on the trans-Siberian railway or in the hulls of ships holding the freezing and diseased. In Magadan alone maybe one and a half million people died, maybe more. Yet here are men and women who survived by faith and show us how evil did not conquer them.

So we must remember. We must listen to their stories and share in their suffering. The pain in my heart has grown for these 10 years of serving the 'repressed' (a word in Russian that is used to describe those who suffered in the camps). This pain carries the mark of tragedy but more than that it carries the mark of triumph. It is the Cross. These interviews are the stories of the Cross.

God has given me the privilege here in far-east Siberia of serving these martyrs of Magadan, these witnesses of faith. I have been forever enriched and have fallen in love with the Cross of Christ because of them and their stories.

Olga said: "At night as soon as the door to our cell opened and someone was led out to be interrogated, the rest of us started praying. We prayed passionately with confidence in the power of love, the power of God, to save us." May I learn – may we learn – from them how to pray and how to believe in the saving love of God in the midst of our suffering so as to find the triumph of the cross and the power of God's love to save us.

Fr Michael Shields
Pastor of the Church of the Nativity of Jesus
Magadan, Russia

Bronislava Bronislavovna Klimavichute

Born: November 6th 1927
Where: Zukai, Sakiai region
Country: Lithuania
Arrested: July 13th 1948
Sentence: 8 years hard labour
Released: August 1st 1954
Rehabilitated: 1994

I WAS ARRESTED IN 1948. It was the July 13th, the feast of St. Antonas. My older sister's husband was named Antonas, Antoni that is, and we celebrated his name day. Two of his brothers came, as well as two neighbours. And I, of course, helped my sister and spent the night with them.

At four o'clock in the morning they came. Lots of soldiers surrounded the house. They woke everyone up and performed a thorough search, ransacking everything. They shook everything. One came out and said: "Here, I found it. I found anti-Soviet proclamations."

"Is this yours?" they ask.

My sister's husband answers: "No, it is not mine."

Of course, they had thrown these papers about themselves and then made it look as if they found them. Neither my sister nor I had been involved in anything like that. We worked on our own farm. I was 20 years old. They had planted all of this. They took us, of course – me, my sister's husband, and his two brothers. I tried to save my family at the interrogation. I was not involved in anything, so I just asserted that we were completely uninvolved. Nor did I admit to what they tried to accuse me of.

15

That is what was happening among us at that time. If they needed to accuse a person in order to imprison him, to put it briefly, they fabricated such situations. And this was all done by Lithuanians themselves. How would the Russians know where to go and whom to take away? Our own countrymen did it. It was their handiwork.

They became mad at my sister's husband because back then there was no vodka to be found anywhere. And he had made some moonshine. It was there in the barn where the cattle stood, so that there would be something for his name day celebration. They had already swept through the village. There were these detachments, a kind of armed band that went around the yards. Two kilometres from us stood a village council. They already knew everything from the locals. They would come and say: "Last night your dog barked. Are you hiding someone?"

They came. They climbed everywhere and found this cask. They smirked, but didn't say anything to Antonas. And they waited until it was ready so that he'd bring it to them. But Antonas did not do this. Well, if you do not do it, then we will do it for you. In the morning at four o'clock, they took us, my sister's husband, his two brothers, and me – the four of us. Everything was ransacked at my parents' house too. My brothers-in-law were immediately released but Antonas and I remained.

To remember the next four days is frightening – a nightmare, especially the nights! We were taunted constantly for four days and nights! Later we were thrown into some cattle yard and separated. Between the boards in the shed were some cracks that had been stuffed with moss. I pulled out the moss. I could see Antonas lying there, terribly beaten up. When I was dragged and thrown in there, a can with some water was left near me.

I drink a little and call to him: "Are you alive, Antonas?"

He raises his head. "Is it you? Give me a little mouthful of water."

But how can he drink it? So I push a straw through the crack. It is empty and hard. He drinks the water through this straw.

"You saved me." he says. "If I had not drunk that water, I would not have survived. You know, tonight I am thinking of escaping."

* * * * *

16

Even remembering it here and now, my heart trembles. It is a nightmare! On the fifth day the investigation was probably going to close but, towards morning, he managed to take off. There was this broken window which he somehow tore off. Then he climbed over the fence which had three rows of barbed wire on top! Where he got the strength, I do not know, because his hands were all beaten – mine were too. They'd stuck pencils between my fingers and beaten them. Everything was all swollen and bruised.

How could he? Where did he get the strength? Well, nevertheless, he ran away. I listened – he was climbing the fence. I listened – and he jumped. I was trembling all over from fear. And then this terrible sound of shooting arose.

July had started. The rye was already high and the forest was not far from there. And he ran away. My parents and sister were shaken after this, especially my sister. She said: "He did not come home." Of course he went home, where else could he go? To go into the woods was certain death. He hid there in the rye near the house. Every night the house was guarded. They tried to discover where he was. They pressed and they pressed. She said: "He did not come back." Well, he hid for two weeks.

Then an order was issued that if he gave himself up, he would be forgiven. What else was there to do? He went and gave himself up. If he went to the forest, he would vanish anyway. If these people did not kill you, others would. What else could happen? My sister could be taken somewhere, exiled to Siberia.

Still, they began to drag him in every day. He was forced to sell his house. It was a good house, brand new. And he bribed them with food and drink every day. And they responded: "Well, Antonas, you should have done this from the very beginning. You yourself are to blame." Such were the times.

* * * * *

My interrogation went like this: I was held there locally for four days. I was beaten and flogged terribly. From there, having been flogged so that I could not walk, I was taken to the city where further interrogation was carried out. But I had been so severely beaten that they could not conduct the interrogation right away. My insides had been pummelled and crushed. Everything was fractured. I'd been thrown on the ground and three or four people would stomp on me with their feet. They had to summon the

17

military doctor. There in the office I was completely undressed and checked out. I was black and blue all over. On one side there was a large bump. My arms were bruised. Everything was swollen. Luckily, the doctor forbade them to interrogate me.

For three weeks they did not come for me at all. They let me lie there. Well, I was young; everything healed – forgive me – like on a dog. The interrogations resumed for another month. My interrogator was so cruel. Komolov was his surname – a Russian. I will never forget him. However, he only tortured me psychologically, not physically. He put me in the corner the whole day.

I stand there and he shouts: "Talk! Talk! Talk!"

But what can I say when there is nothing for me to say? How can I slander myself or other people? Should I pull down another 20 people with me? I cannot do that! So I stand in the corner.

He is now exhausted. He is completely angry. He goes out, smokes, returns, and again: "Well, sit. Sit. Now talk!"

Well, what can I say? What?! I begin to tremble all over. It is impossible to tremble so.

I could not even talk. Yes, and everything was so bruised. And I had diarrhoea almost all the time. I shout through the translator: "I need a toilet!"

"Take her out," he says, "this whore." He only ever refers to me as a whore. "Take away this whore."

I also could not eat, because everything inside hurt so. Everything hurt so badly! Oh, Lord, have mercy! What, after all, was this for? I do not know why. I was 22 when I was arrested.

They brought forth various eyewitnesses against me. Of course, I had never seen any of them before. How could I have said something to them?

So I said that I did not know them. Apparently, they did not get anything from me.

Two months passed and I was sent to a large prison in Mariampol. It was a very large prison. They gathered people there from the whole region, and our region was large.

I was held in prison for a year. I was brought to trial four times – four times!

They'd bring me and we'd sit there in a pre-trial cell. "Your witnesses did not come." Well, what kind of witness could there have been? Where were these witnesses from?

Papa and Mama hired a lawyer. He came and spoke with me a little. How could he help in political cases? He couldn't do anything. So I was brought to the courthouse and back four times for trial. I was held there the whole winter. That's how I sat out 1947 – in prison.

At the end of the summer of 1948, either in July or August – the rye was already high – they brought me for a second round of interrogations, again to the same investigator, Komolov. What's a year sitting in a prison cell with 30 people?! All kinds of women were there – the educated and wise. We came from every educational background.

The investigator says to me: "So, you've come."

I answer: "I've come because I was brought."

"Well, sit and tell me about it."

"What? I'm not going to tell you anything new."

"I see you've already passed through the university."
"They don't teach any special lessons, but I managed to pick up something." I speak to him like that now. I am not afraid of him. I was brought to him.

"Tell me!"

I answer: "You can write what you want, but I'm not telling you anything new – not a thing!"

"Then repeat what you've already said."

"You have everything written down. I've already forgotten everything."

"You whore! You won't forget it not until the end of your days. You'll never forget it."

Indeed, he was right. You never forget.

Even though he beat and bullied others, at least he didn't do that to me except with words. And he never deprived me of any parcels my family sent. It's possible, of course, that the doctor told him not to deprive me since I was so thin and emaciated and all bruised. But I will never forget those words.

And so they returned me to the large prison.

* * * * *

It was already late autumn when suddenly I was summoned.

"Sign here. You've been sentenced."

"Who sentenced me?"

"A special commission in Moscow, the Supreme Troika. Sign."

"I will not sign. I don't know who sentenced me or when."

It was all the same to them whether I signed or not. It didn't matter.

* * * * *

We were sent by transport to a transit camp in Vilnius, in Lithuania. There a large transport of prisoners was being gathered. And so we were brought there. This was at the end of October, because when they brought us to Mordovia, to the Pot'ma station, there was snow already. There were large political prison camps in Mordovia. Everywhere in the forest there was one camp after another.

There we were assigned to work. I was immediately sent to the sewing factory – and I can't sew at all! I don't like such work. Besides, my heart was not well at that time. As soon as I sat at one of those machines, I became ill. I began to fall. I'd sit and work, and right away, no matter what, I would start to feel bad and I'd fall over.

20

I worked on an assembly line. The shirt began at one end of the shop and finished at the other. The operations were divided up. At first I was made an apprentice, but then seeing that I was ill and I was having difficulty learning this skill, they sat me down to sew buttons. So I spent the first winter in that shop.

Then in the summer we all were sent to the collective farm, at Camp Outpost number 13 near the Pot'ma station. The farming was done in the forest. That is, the forest had been burned down. All around were tree stumps, branches, and roots. We collected them. We dug with shovels. And then we planted cabbages, potatoes, and carrots. And do you know, by autumn simply enormous potatoes had grown! It was amazing what a harvest we had that autumn.

Towards the autumn we were asked who knew how to cut hay. Well, I had grown up on a farm and could do all that. My father had taught me a lot. Besides, they gave those who cut a little larger ration; for example we would get a little more milk. It was still slavery, of course, but still it's something better to remember.

Then trouble hit – I caught malaria. The disease raged there. It simply mowed people down. Your temperature goes to over 104 degrees Fahrenheit. The winter was nothing, but in the summer when the hot weather began... I remember now and I wonder how I survived!

We'd be led into the field in the raging heat. The guards stood on the edge of the field and commanded: "Work!" Lunch was brought and we ate it there under the blazing sun in the middle of the field. There was no cover. We were forbidden to go anywhere and then we returned to work.

Well, my temperature would rise over 104 degrees Fahrenheit. Then I would look for some sort of ditch. I would lay, buried, in it. I remember one time a guard came up to me and said – I was beginning to understand a little Russian by then, which up until then I'd understood very little of – "Here," he said, "you'll die there.

"Bury yourself here and no one will recognise you, not your mother, not your father."

It made no difference to me, I was feeling so bad. In the evening the girls were led back, and I was taken immediately to the medical unit. I was given medicine for malaria, Akhrikin, but I became so yellow from it. It was simply terrifying. So I was kept in the hospital for a little bit and then again sent back to work. It was like that till autumn; only in the autumn did the illness abate. So in the autumn and winter you're not sick. The doctor, also a prisoner, told me that if I changed climate, then the disease would go away as a consequence, and so it happened. When I was sent to Kolyma, I was no longer troubled by malaria.

Thus passed 1949 to 1950. In the spring a new, large transport was organised and we were brought to Kolyma. It took a whole month to get to Vanino Bay.

* * * * *

And there at Vanino Bay, we endured evil. These rogues, thieves, and rapists practically cut us up. We had barely arrived when the supervisor hurried us along: "Girls," – he only called us girls. He never insulted us. We met humane people among them too – "Girls, hurry up. As soon as we finish registering you this evening, we can no longer protect you. Try to be quicker." He even warned us that we might be attacked. We hurried. We were unloaded and taken to the bathhouse, then for sanitary processing. While we bathed, everything was done. Our guards handed us over. Other guards took us. But the criminals had just come out. "Oh, we'll have work to do tonight!" they threatened. We were so frightened; we huddled together in a corner of the tent. Yes, we had been put in tents. These tents somehow stood apart. Even the supervisors did not go there at night. They were scared of these mongrels, who went around dressed so flashily. We were amazed. "Good God, just where are these people from? Who are they? And how do they have such good connections?" It turns out they were just "common criminals" – thieves, rapists, and murderers.

Well, we were put in these tents. The supervisor warned us: "Don't all lie down to sleep at once. Have six people per watch just as a precaution." So we pulled up a plank from the bunk and stood guard. Of course, they came. They wanted to knife us. Killing someone did not mean anything to these people. It was just entertainment for them. But that night they couldn't do anything to us. We all got up. What could they do? They just cut the strap on a tent.

The next day the supervisor discovered a note hung on a wire where the men's unit was. It had been thrown over the fence. The common criminals were inviting all their men to help them deal with us the following night. "Come," they said, "and we'll knife them." The supervisor removed the note and came to us. "Quickly get your things and be ready in five minutes," he said.

We were taken six or seven kilometres on foot, right to the very Bay of Vanino. There was, I remember, a heat wave. It was May of 1950. We were put in a former prisoner of war camp. There were these clay houses that had been stuck together without roofs. We were put there and, I don't know why, but we were held there all summer. Why we were there until October, I don't know.

But then in October, we were loaded onto the steamer, the *Miklukho-Maklai*, and brought here to Kolyma. We sailed for nine days. It is terrible to recall. We were with those same criminals. We were given bread; the criminals stole it. The same with our *kasha*. In the Gulf of Tatar, we got caught in a storm and barely survived. When I remember how we sailed – the horror!

We were brought here in the winter. At first we sat at a transit camp at the Fourth Kilometre. They held everyone there in the beginning. It was a quarantine point. They watched to see if anyone got sick with anything. Then we were gathered and taken to cut timber at the 23rd Kilometre mark from the city. This transit camp was called 23/15.

We were taken to cut wood in the dead of winter. And we were housed in tents! The temperatures dropped to minus 58 degrees Fahrenheit and we were housed in tents! In the middle of the tent stood two old kerosene barrels – instead of a stove, you had to stoke these. As long as you stoked them, it was warm. When they burned out, it was just as cold inside the tent as outside. And we'd come back from cutting lumber barely alive. We couldn't sit down. We had to stoke these barrels. Good Lord!

The bunks were thrown together with rounded branches from larch trees. The twigs had not even been cut off particularly well. Nor were we given any sort of mattress or bedding. We'd come back from the forest and our padded pants would be wet. Still, we'd lay them under us for bedding. That was it! We slept like that!

I remember Yana Kolpakaite; she was my friend in the camp. Somehow we were kept together. While I was still home, before my departure to Russia, Mama and Papa had brought me a small broadcloth blanket. So the two of us would huddle next to one another and cover ourselves with this little blanket and then with our wet pea-coats on top. We huddled together like piglets; our pants underneath us. By morning these pants would be dry, but the wool boots would not dry out. We'd placed them near this barrel, but if no one stoked it during the night, what kind of heat would come from it? In the morning we'd get up and what an icebox! We were woken at 5:00. At 5:30 we left for the forest. I don't know – only God could have protected us then. It's a wonder we didn't catch pneumonia.

We suffered in this tent the entire winter. It was only later, the next winter, when we were taken into a *zemlianka*. A *zemlianka* is a hole dug in the ground. There is a roof on top. Inside there are bunks. But in this earthen dug out, it was, of course, warmer. Also that second winter, the head of the camp was changed. One woman, as a result of an unfortunate incident, received a head wound and was taken to Magadan. There she complained and described how we were being treating. The supervisor practically didn't feed us, despite the work. The soup was just water with frozen potatoes floating in it. The *kasha* was just a little water. You couldn't tell whether it was kasha or soup that was being poured. Millet and lentil. I still cannot stand millet.

And so, a big commission came to investigate. They started to do audits. Lord, the rats and the mice had eaten all the good grain! There had been good, wonderful grain after all – rice for instance, but they didn't give us that. The camp supervisor was that cruel a person! Of course, we never knew for sure, but we heard that he was sentenced and given something like 10 years.
So we were put in these earthen dugouts for the second winter and given a new supervisor. He managed to get fish for us and to cook the *kasha* like it was supposed to be. He even added little pieces of fat sometimes – nice!

While we were working, the stoves in the earthen dugouts were stoked by Pani Anna so that they were always kept warm. Everyone had their own little bowl. We would put these bowls on the stove, cook our *kasha* with lard, and even bake in them. Oh, everything was rosy. We'd come in and everything would be hot and so tasty. So at least we were fed a little better the second winter. For those who had survived, it was now a little easier.

Of course, we were forced to work very hard. We had a squad of six people and we were supposed to produce 18 cubic metres of lumber every day. I worked with Maria Sobol. We cut wood together. She is now Maria Trubi.

Somehow she came and said: "Well, where can I find a good partner who can cut wood well?" Of course, it was very important to find a good partner. It made work much easier. I kept quiet. How would I know if I was any good with a saw? But she suggested: "Bronislava, let's you and I give it a try." And so we began to work together, cutting trees in the forest. We worked well together. It was easy for us to work together.

We always tried to fulfil our quota of 18 cubic metres. Mary and I cut and cut, and then sawed the logs into two metre lengths. Others would trim the branches, and still others would stack them up into huge piles for approval. The brigade leader would measure the stacks and approve them.

We tried to fulfil the quota quickly so that we could come back just a little earlier and rest. We would rest and then line up at the mess hall. Three people would be chosen to clean potatoes for the administration at night. Potatoes were cooked only for the camp administration. I would come back from logging and stand in line. The kitchen was also in a basement in a dugout. We'd form a line by the door and wait. The cook would open the door and choose: "You come in. You come in."

She didn't take everyone, but for some reason she always took me. Not everyone was needed. The rest would leave. Whoever ended up there would bring her little bowl with her. And we'd clean potatoes until four in the morning. The potatoes were so tiny and small. Good Lord, we'd clean. We'd nod off, but it was impossible to dream. Well, they'd cook these potatoes and put some in our bowls for us. They'd also give a little piece of bread. We were now full. I'd give my portion of *kasha* to Jana. And she'd be full that day. Then in the morning, back to work again. The next evening Jana would go to the mess hall. This time she'd clean potatoes at night and give me her ration.

How beautifully Jana sang! Yes, she sang very beautifully. We were friends for a long time after our release. She moved with her husband to Lithuania. We wrote back and forth for a long time. She was so good. She'd clean potatoes and sing. She sang everywhere. She was always singing. We'd go to work, from work – she'd be singing!

I ask her: "Jana, where do you get the strength?"

"Ah, when you sing, it is easier on the soul! Pray and it will be easier."

"Just how much can you pray?!"

"Well, the Our Father, the Hail Mary – and you've prayed. How much do you need to pray?"

That was Jana. She was very good – not a dejected person!

* * * * *

The camp at the 23/15 Kilometre did not have its own bakery. And when a blizzard raged, we were often completely without bread for weeks. When there was no bread, they gave the same broth, just liquid. You couldn't call it *kasha*, just slop. It was very difficult. Bread was delivered for us only to the 23rd Kilometre, to the village of Snezhnaia. There was a booth there. Firewood was brought there on tractors. A vehicle would come bringing the bread. But if there was too much snow, the vehicle did not drive any further. Only a tractor could get through. And when it was completely drifted over with snow, then even the tractor could not get through. Then they'd rouse us at night, organise a brigade, and send us 15 kilometres for the bread. Of course, this was cruelty to be chased out at night for bread after such hard work.

Still we'd have to go. There was no road and the snow was very deep. We'd have to guess where the path was. We couldn't walk. We would drag ourselves along. Whoever was first carved a path through the snow. Going first was the hardest job. She'd go and go until she'd worn herself out, then she'd go to the end. The next girl would move up to the front. So we'd drag ourselves along in the tracks. And until it was your turn to carve out the path, you'd walk and sleep. You'd really sleep! Imagine – you walk, and you're sleeping. You can even dream! It is difficult to believe, but it's true. I experienced this myself. We slept on the move.

We'd arrive there. They'd give us sacks with frozen loaves of bread. Before we could carry it all the way back, it would already be crushed in the sacks. It'd be just bread crumbs. We'd carry five or six loaves in sacks on our shoulders. Well, how can you bear this – carrying bread on your back when you yourself are so hungry! Oh, how it smells! You don't have the strength to bear it! So you'd make a small hole in the sack and you'd eat at least some frozen bread crumbs. Whoever had a conscience would eat just these crumbs, but some people would finish it all while carrying it back. Hardly any bread would remain for us. They'd give us crumbs in a small bowl. There would be no more bread, because someone had already eaten it all.

Whole brigades were formed with people from the Baltics. Maria Sobol was from Belarus, but the rest of the brigade was Lithuanian. And the regimen was, of course, very strict, like in a concentration camp. You'd work until you fell down. And whoever fell down and could not walk any more was taken away to Magadan. And there they would die in the prisoners' hospital. The weakest were not kept with us. It was a work zone.

* * * * *

We all had numbers sewn on our backs, pants and jacket. We all lived under these numbers. My very first number that was given to me is now in the church. It hangs in the Chapel of the Repressed, under the Cross – Fr Michael asked me for it. Even back then I thought that I would keep it. This was the very first number, which they wrote with their own hands and gave to me. The next ones, when that was torn or worn out, we had to write and sew ourselves. During such hard work in the woods and dirt, it would, after all, quickly be worn out. We'd find some sort of scrap of cloth, write out the number with a chemical pencil and sew it on our back and pants. If you didn't do it in time and it began to look bad, you were sent to the punishment cell. Yes! You didn't have any rights to a name and surname. I was D2-129. That was the only way I could address a supervisor. It was my first, middle and last name.

* * * * *

In the spring of 1952 there were rumours that those with short sentences – under 10 years, and I had eight years, the very shortest – would leave the *Berlag* for Special Forced Labour Camps. That's where there were not only political prisoners, but all different types of criminals.
At that time, I was experiencing another problem; my blood pressure was over 200. Good God, I felt bad. My bunk was on the third tier, up high. I could barely climb down from there, my blood pressure was so high. At the medical unit I was told that I would be included on a list of those who should be sent back to the mainland. I couldn't be kept here on account of my health. The list came and I was summoned. Good God, I couldn't really believe it.

We were gathered up again and brought here to Magadan to the 4th Kilometre transit camp. We were formed up and told: "Rip off your numbers." We were frightened. Were they going to shoot us? We ripped the numbers off of one another's backs and everywhere else and were settled in this transit camp. We weren't held there for long. Again we were put in formation. The camp administration arrived. They were called buyers. They began to select people from among us for work. The weakest were not taken. Those who were stronger, who looked more or less healthy, were taken.

Who was chosen? Mainly Lithuanians, Latvians, Estonians and Ukrainians. We workers – in reality, slaves – were again sent to cut lumber, me included, despite my high blood pressure. Well, I was young. The regimen became a little easier. It went away little by little.

And again we cut timber at the 47th Kilometre. This place was called Okhra. It was the command centre for all the guards in the Magadan camps. We cut timber, carried it, and stacked it in piles. But it was a free regimen. Guards did not follow us everywhere. Only one supervisor checked our work. And we began to receive a little bit of money. We could now buy ourselves a little piece of bread. Every month we were allowed to sign out 100 roubles, for example. And now it was a little easier for us.

Oh, what a large forest we cut! The trees were enormous. A thick, tall forest stood where the 31st Quadrant is now. And a large camp, the most enormous camp, was there. And where the leather factory is, there was a large pig farm.

We cut these trees all winter and spring, until summer. In the summer we were taken to cut hay at Serdiak, near Ola. Gadlia was on one side and Serdiak on the other. There was an outpost there. I was taken. I was there for a long time. In the summer we cut hay and put it in stacks in the forest.

We work in groups of six. We cut. One girl works on the bunching rake. She drags it behind us. Then we put it in stacks.

The supervisor comes and checks. "Girls, everything is here."

Of course, it is here. What else could we do? Everyone is here. There is nowhere to go.

And such fresh air! Quiet all around! And berries – blueberries – honeysuckle of the sea.

We, of course, took this to heart. We worked. We produced tonnage, and we did it ourselves. We were almost independent; we were almost free.

In the winter I was assigned to horses. In the summer we stacked hay. In the winter we transported the hay with horses. And during the winter in the morning, we left for the forest at four o'clock and around five or six in the evening we came back with a whole load of hay, eight or nine carts of hay.

* * * * *

Then all of a sudden, in August of 1954, I was summoned and released! I was given a certificate and told: "Be well."

No one offered me anything.

If you want to go home, go. If you want to settle here somewhere, ok.

At this time many, many prisoners began to be freed. Both girls and men began to be released. We were completely without guards! I thought: "I've been freed and I'll go home."

But then our Lithuanians introduced me to my future husband. He still had five years loss of political and civil rights to go. He was forbidden to leave. In tears he persuaded me to stay and marry him. Then my daughter, Berutochka, was born. It was difficult, very difficult as we started our life together. We were hungry all the time and we suffered much.

At that time no one would give me a job. Wherever they were supposedly hiring, I'd go, but they'd look in my passport – there was a note in it that I had served eight years – and that was the end of it. They'd say there was a condition in my passport and they wouldn't take me. And we had a baby too! When I was asked about my family situation, I would answer honestly: "Yes, I have a small child."

"Oh no, no work!"

I wanted to get a job in the hospital. There was a woman in the cadre office. Oh, how I begged her!

"Take me! Put me on a waiting list! I need to work!"

"No, no, no!"

So many people began to be released after the death of Stalin! Even if someone had to leave, they immediately took another person for his place.

29

So I suffered and suffered. I walked and walked, and fell ill with hepatitis. I was put in the hospital. My husband had to sit at home with the baby. I said to the doctor: "We are dying of hunger. If I have to lie to here, my husband has to sit at home." I lay there for just eight days all together. I cried. I prayed. I was sent home, but I hadn't really healed!

While I was in the infectious diseases wing, I saw Maria Trubi. I had cut timber with her. She worked in that wing. She praised me to the head of the department, Valeriia Aleksandrovna, and to the senior nurse. And Lidia worked there. She had to leave and so I was able to take her place. Thus I worked there for 19 years. The girls in the x-ray department wanted me to come to work there, but Valeriia Aleksandrovna said: "Where are you going with your ill liver?" So I stayed. They kept me on as a simple worker. And so long as the head of the department was there, I could not leave. She would not let me go. So I worked until I retired.

* * * * *

So life passed. I did not know my youth, nor my young adulthood. My life was terribly hard. I had my childhood, of course. We had a very good family. My parents were poor peasants, but such hard workers. There were two of us children. I never asked Mama, but my older sister told me that several other children had died. She survived. She was the oldest, the first. And I was the last, the unfortunate one. There was 15 years difference between us. Two of us remained alive.

* * * * *

The first time I took a trip after I had started working was in 1959. By that time I had not seen my family for somewhere around 14 years. After my illness, I was thin and yellow. But how joyous this reunion was! What a good, joyous holiday it was! It was the first time I felt really human. My Mama died in 1965, my Papa in 1968.

* * * * *

There was a very strong tradition of religious upbringing in our family. We were raised in religion from childhood itself. Whether you wanted to or not, you were put on your knees to pray morning and evening prayers. Papa taught us to pray. "You need to put your hands like this and that's how you

30

pray to God, only on your knees! Lord, Heavenly Father – ask only like that!"

We celebrated all the feast days in the evenings. Papa sang well. He was invited to participate on feast days and to sing at funerals. In the evenings Mama would come and Papa would sing. Mama would respond to him: "How good!" And later we also said evening prayers together.
In the spring, in the month of May, we prayed the Litany to the Mother of God – this was essential! We gathered at someone's house with the whole village. For example, we'd sing at my sister's. We didn't just say the prayer, we sang it. Then we went on.

In our village there were three huge crosses. And early, early in the morning, when the sun would just begin to rise, everyone would gather at the first cross. They would sing and pray. They would sing the litany and the psalms. They would sing, and then they would go to the second cross. There they would sing all that was necessary. They would go to the third cross and sing there too. And so every day, every month. It was called praying at the crosses! Then everyone would depart, each to his own work.

In the evening, we would gather at someone's house, whoever's hut was a little bigger. In each house hung an icon of the Mother of God, very beautifully decorated. Candles would burn. We would sing the whole litany. And in June we gathered and sang the Litany of Jesus. We gathered all the time. It was good and friendly.

Faith helped everyone to survive in life – only faith! I, for example, I know the Rosary, the Litany of the Mother of God, by heart from camp. Tired, I would go from work. I would bow my head just a little when I prayed. It was forbidden – they didn't allow it. And we would say all our prayers on the road! I would walk and I would pray to myself. Oh, how I prayed. I would pray the Litany on the way to work and coming back from work. While we marched, I would pray. If we were working on the roads – we were sent to guard, to meet, or to accompany vehicles when a blizzard raged – I would pray the Rosary the whole time. If we walked far, we would say the Rosary. Only prayers – of course! – only prayers saved me. In prayers, there was unending help. We prayed together in the dugouts and we tried to gather to pray on feast days.

And now I only live for our church. After all, for me this is everything now. This is my family, my support. These are my friends and my prayers. This is now the dearest thing to me.

When I found this church, I cried. In 1991, I was listening to the radio and they announced: "Catholic service in the club at the Avtotek."
I listened once to the announcement and a second time. I thought: "Something is not right. It can't be." Up until then I had not gone to church in Magadan, although there was an Orthodox church. I had dropped by a couple of times, but it was not my Church. The ceremony was not the same. The liturgy was different.

When I was still working I always walked from work, from the hospital to Marchekan, deliberately. I would walk and I would pray. I would pray the Rosary. I would pray a litany. I would recite all the prayers while walking home.

When I hear that announcement for a third time, I think: "Well, I will go and see." I go and as soon as I see Fr Augustine in our Catholic vestments, I think: "Gracious God, this is really our priest."

And when he performs the liturgy, I cry. "This is just like it was in Lithuania. This is ours." I cry through the whole liturgy. The priest wants to talk with me, but I say that I am so anxious that day that I can't. "Today I cannot." I am so anxious.

And I begin to go to church. It is so good. Then I take a trip and when I get back, I go to the club, but the guard stops me.

"They no longer meet here."

And some time passes before I find out that they are meeting at 25 Proletarskaia Street. And so I go to find it.

I find it.

And once I find it, I never go anywhere else. I have found our Church!

* * * * *

I want to say this about the meetings of the repressed; about the teas which they provide for us – it is wonderful! There is the chance to see each other at least, to socialise. People meet, talk and share. None of my fellow

32

countrymen are there. Almost none of them stayed behind in Magadan. But many Ukrainians remained. Take Olga; how many fellow countrymen she has! It is very good.

For so many years no one noticed us. Now I see the hearts of people warm up. In the beginning these people did not come, they were more constrained, untrusting. But now it is different. Before, many who came to church had not been baptised, now almost everyone is. This is good, especially for the elderly. At this age, you need to deeply understand everything; to acknowledge all of your past and the importance of communion with God.

* * * * *

How did my rehabilitation happen? Immediately after *perestroika* I received my rehabilitation from Lithuania, but I was not given a supplement to my pension for my rehabilitation. For a while my daughter, Berutochka, did not insist that I try to obtain it. She began to insist when it began to affect her. She lived in the village Omolon, on the border, and the KGB began to say to her: "Your mother is not rehabilitated." My daughter said to me: "Mama, go; go. After all, you are rehabilitated by Lithuania; Russia too should acknowledge it after all..."

Then she sent me a newspaper article about a decree by President Yelstin which said that if someone was rehabilitated in a republic, then Russia should acknowledge it. Russia should also rehabilitate the person.

I heard that the writer Sandler worked with the repressed and helped them. So I went to him and he listened to me. I told him my whole saga. He answered me: "Well, you see, your Lithuanian lawyers do not acknowledge our Russian law. That is why Russia does not recognise you."

How offensive it was to me to hear these words, as if this was all illegal – this rehabilitation paper and the documents that I brought to him! I bit my lip so as not to cry. I walked home and cried the whole way there with such an ache in my heart. But somehow it calmed me that Yeltsin had issued a decree saying that Russia acknowledged a rehabilitation from a republic. Sandler had advised me to go to the procurator's office and had given me the address of the Magadan procurator. But I had waved my hand.

"I will not go anywhere! Oh, the years I have lived through!"

It was so offensive, so offensive. I cried. "They will not admit it! They will not recognise it!"

And then Berutochka came to visit. She persuaded me, took me by the hand, and led me to Dzerzhinskii Street, to the Magadan KGB office. The guard asked what business we were there on. He wrote everything down. Then he led us to the basement where their archives are. There we filled out a request form. I was told that if I had a rehabilitation from Lithuania, then a decision should be made within two weeks. And within two weeks I received a notice to come and get my documents. We went and received this same confirmation, only it was now in Russian. It meant that at last I was fully rehabilitated.

And that was that. How quickly they were able to decide everything, but, oh, the humiliation that I had had to endure!

I remember the words of my first investigator, Komolov. "You," he said, "will never forget this until the end of your life."

It turns out that he was right.

Olga Alekseievna Gureeva

Born:	October 25th 1928
Where:	Roshniv, Tismenitskii region, Ivano-Frankiv'ska Oblast'
Country:	Ukraine
Arrested:	December 5th 1945
Sentence:	25 years of hard labour plus 5 years loss of rights and exile
Released:	March 1956
Rehabilitated:	1993

ON DECEMBER 5th 1945, a whole platoon of soldiers with two tanks rode into our village. Many people were killed that day.

They came into our home and simply began pillaging. They took everything that was there – clothing, livestock, grain. They used physical force. Yes, they terrorised us.

* * * * *

Up to that time I had studied for just three months at an educational institute. I had only just turned 18. My 15-year-old brother and I were taken away. The entire day they interrogated us. They took us in turn and tried to somehow find even the smallest association with the partisans. During the investigation, I was severely beaten. Yes, they employed the most frightening physical tortures. Towards evening we were taken away to the oblast. They were afraid to remain in the village at night. My brother was also taken with me. He vanished.

We were brought to the prison in Ivano-Frankiv'sk. We were not allowed to bring anything with us, not even a comb or a toothbrush. For the first few days, I was put in an isolation cell. Later, after the first interrogation, I was brought to a cell where there were so many people that it was difficult to even sit. The cells were all overcrowded. There were only young people. They had taken everyone, everyone in succession. But from my village no one else except me and my brother were taken, I think because I did not admit to anything. I refused to say anything when they questioned me in the village. I did not understand why I should put people in prison if I had no ties with them except as neighbours. Later they began to accuse me of contact with nationalists. The investigation was very hard since I did not corroborate anything which they tried to accuse me of. On the whole they interrogated me at night, using physical force. It went on for four months.

In the cells there were so many people that we were all packed, like herring, in two rows. The cells were narrow. Everyone lay on her side. If someone's side began to hurt, then absolutely everyone had to turn. Besides this, the floor was bare. It was very painful.

Not everyone was brought out to be interrogated right away. We were summoned in turn. When someone was taken, everyone else knelt and prayed, and prayed until she came back. When she returned, then we thanked to God that she had returned.

They employed the most frightening tortures and beatings. When I was returned, I would be half-dead, black, beaten up like a piece of meat. All this at the age of 18!

In tears, we all prayed. How we asked the Lord and the Mother of God to help us endure those trials! I think that all that could only be endured with God's help. No one thought about freedom. No one walked out of there. Everyone waited for the end of the interrogation and sentencing. My investigation finished after four months. I was forced to sign a confession. We signed not because we were guilty, but so that they would stop torturing us. And most girls, from both the city and the village, were not guilty. They did not know anything. But they took everything upon themselves just to be left alone. They could not hold up to torture.

When I was at last summoned for trial, everything had already been decided and judged. They immediately announced my sentence – 20 years of hard labour, five years loss of rights and exile. The troika sentenced me. The sentence sounded like this: "Article 54, betrayal of the motherland, and Article 54.11a, participant in a Ukrainian nationalist organisation." They offered me a chance to say my last wish. I said that I only wished to see my family. "I do not want anything else."

They answered, "Fine." But my parents were already bound for Siberia. They had been already exiled by this time, but I did not know anything and they did not tell me.

* * * * *

So began a different life – the road to Siberia. I had been arrested in December; now in May we were led with dogs to the station in Lviv, to go on to the transit camp. On the road an acquaintance shouted to me that my parents had been taken to Siberia. That is how we lost each other.

It was May 9th 1945 – Victory Day – and we were in transport to Lviv. We were loaded into dirty, fetid cattle cars. We travelled for a month and nine days. A wooden pipe, with a diameter about the size of the palm of your hand, was put in the car for our needs. We were given two small pieces of bread and dried fish to eat. Water, which was not even always clean, was given to us in a beaten-up cup. We had to wash, bathe and drink with just this little cup of water. There was no other water.

We travelled to Irkutsk in these cars. During the day we were herded into a dead end at a station and during the night we travelled. We were enemies of the people and people treated us in different ways. One might insult us; but another would take pity.

So we reached Novosibirsk. There we were led to the bathhouse. I was very sick. I nearly died on the road, I was so ill. And in the bathhouse, I lost consciousness. When I regained consciousness, a soldier stood above me with a raised boot. For some reason I remember that I said: "Why did you wake me? I felt so good." They wanted to leave me there, but the girls shouted and would not give up on me. They took me under their arms to the car and we went on.

We were brought to the transit camp in Taishet. There were only young people among us, aged from 15 to 30 years old. The majority were Ukrainians. We were all very tired and emaciated. Here they began to sort us. I was counted as an invalid, and we, a group of sick and worn out people, were sent by foot along the road through the *taiga* to the Irkutsk Oblast, 130 kilometres from Taishet. It took a week to walk to the camp. We were so weak. We did not know where they were taking us. We lived in another world, where no one ever said where they were taking us, why, or for how long.

When we were about 30 kilometres from the camp, we were herded into some kind of barn, by a fence near the guardhouse, to spend the night. It was now June and already warm. The flowers had bloomed; everywhere was green with life. There was a lot of straw and we simply rested in the straw, having been tormented by the bedbugs in the barracks, which had swarmed over us and callously gnawed at us.

In the middle of the night, we suddenly heard another group of people arrive. They began a roll call very loudly and we could hear that they were men. We immediately began to protest. We shouted to the guard that we were not going to sleep next to men. We were very frightened. We began to cry. We thought that they were common criminals. But a man's voice answered us: "Girls sleep peacefully. We do not need anyone." The men were led in. They all fell into silence. No one spoke – they had no strength.

And when they woke us for roll call in the morning and led the men away, we saw that they were living corpses. They were like ghosts. They were shadows of men – grey faces, grey people, completely lifeless in torn pea-coats and caps with ear-flaps in the middle of summer. They were invalids, who had been sentenced in the 1930s.

It is impossible to believe it if you did not see it with your own eyes. We women were escorted by dogs and guards. But the invalids – men! – hardly moved forward. They supported each other. They would fall and get up. They fell before our eyes and died. And some medical assistant went and squeamishly felt their pulse. He would throw them by the leg away on the edge of the road. A cart went behind to pick up the dead. To see that was horrible.

Later we arrived at the camp outpost. A road had been hacked through the *taiga*. On the left side were just camps. The men were taken to the side. One of them said: "Girls, this is the last time we will go down this path. We will not return from here."

I remember that one of them rebelled. The convoy guard raised the butt of his weapon. We were forced to lie down on the ground with our faces down. You could hear someone shout: "Girls, remember we are not traitors." When we stood up, there was a pool of blood and that was all. It was forbidden to say even a word. The men were led away and we went on. It was very frightening. We cried. We prayed. And we walked into the unknown. We walked for a whole week. We slept along the road to the camps. There were people there in these camps, but we never saw them.

* * * * *

Finally, we arrived in our camp, which was called Kon'iaki. There had never been anyone in this camp before us. The head of the camp greeted us well. He said: "Get settled. Tomorrow you will go to pick swede. The swede plants are still very small, but growing thickly. If you can, then gather and eat them. And if there is enough to fill small sacks, take them, because I have nothing else, no provisions, no clothing."

At breakfast we would be given a small piece of bread – 14 ounces. It was such a small piece of almost raw dough. Sometimes there would be soup made from some dead, fetid fish. I could not bear the smell and did not go into the mess hall. I lived on just hot water and a small piece of bread, oh, and on the swede.

Most frightening of all were the midges. They blocked out the sun. There was no rescue from it. We were given pants with a little string to hold them up, and shirts. A man brought us buckets of tar. We rubbed it on our face, hands, and legs. We made crowns from grass for our head and also poured tar on them. But all of this did little to save us from the midges.

Later the swede grew quite large. The convoy guard that led us were old men. Sometimes we would approach the field where the swede was. We would walk in rows of five. The convoy guard would say: "Brigade, get in two lines. March quickly to the swede. Take as much as you can." And when we arrived at the work site, there was the command: "Sit. Eat the swede." We would begin to eat. "And now, sing." We would sing and then in one voice, we would cry. The command came: "Stand!" And then we went back to work. Towards autumn, after we had harvested the crops, we were sent back by foot to the main camp in Taishet again.

* * * * *

So, we arrived in Taishet. There was a men's camp. God, how thin and horrible they were. We would go into the mess hall. We were given soup and the men would surround us and beg: "Perhaps you will not eat it all?" How can you eat when a person stands there starving? We gave it away to them. We, after all, can endure more than men.

In Taishet, there was a very large transit camp – thousands and thousands of prisoners, exhausted, sick, hungry, and tattered, like shadows. A transport of prisoners was gathered, then we were loaded again in cattle cars and sent... no one knew where. We were brought to the Mariinski camps, Kemorovskaia Oblast, to a transit camp 70 kilometres outside the city. This was late autumn 1945. Again there was a sorting. This procedure was always very difficult. We were kept outside while everyone, all their documents and sentences were reviewed, regardless of the weather. We were all so ragged and thin that our clothes nearly fell off.

We – the hard labourers, strict regimers, Article 58ers – were kept separately. We were taken in trucks with 30 people and 3 soldiers, through the steppe, all uninhabited, and then suddenly there was a camp. 'Merchants' – those fat-bellied brass of various ranks, who would select us according to our ability for work – were already waiting for us. We women – we were really just children – and some elderly women were taken. This was a large strict regime camp. How many victims it held I do not know. For the women there was a very long barrack, divided into sections, and fenced off. The barrack was enclosed by a high fence. The men were kept separately.

For the first week the weather was still favourable. It was still warm and we were sent to dig up potatoes. The potatoes were large, but forage, not suitable for people to eat. They were intended for processing and the brewing of alcohol. We did not look in such bad shape because during the summer we had got a little stronger. But within a week it became sharply colder. Snow fell. Freezing cold set in. Blizzards began that went on without end. The camp did not have any communication with the outside world. We were no longer let out anyway, because we were completely unclothed. We had nothing – practically no clothing. And the whole winter we were kept in the zone in the camp. We lay on the bunks the whole time. For a week or more there would be no bread, no salt. The food was prepared without salt from frozen potatoes, cabbage and rotting herring. The food was brought in metal cans from the men's zone. It was passed under the gate – "Take it." But we were never allowed out to fetch it.

We would ask: "And the bread?"

"There is no bread." And again we went back to our bunks.

We reached the point that we were suffering dystrophia. We were horrible to look at, like ancient old women. I was even more frightening than I am now! Young girls looked like real old women. When we were weighed in the spring, I was 83 pounds. It looked like you could play the xylophone on my ribs. So those were the first eight months we spent in the bunks. This was in the camp 70 kilometres from Mariinsk. It was called Novoivanovka, but people called this place the Valley of Death or the Devil's Canyon. For many months terrible blizzards blew and so no provisions were brought in. And the locals had no reserves.

There were two sisters, Elena Arsent'ievna and Marfa Arsent'ievna Marchenko, from Dnepropetrovsk in the barrack with us. Both were doctors. They worked in the men's zone. They told us what was happening there - it was nothing more than a hospital. There were epidemics of typhus, dysentery and tuberculosis. People were dying not by the tens, but by the hundreds. Our barrack stood on a rise and we could watch what went on outside from the upper bunk. Every day we saw vehicles loaded with dead bodies, just like wood, not covered with anything. At the guardhouse, the vehicles were stopped and thoroughly searched to check that no one alive had hidden in there.

For many months we lived completely cut off from the whole world. No one saw even a scrap of newspaper – or even ordinary paper. Of course, correspondence was not allowed. Even the camp officials had to post messages on small, well-cleaned boards. We passed the time in prayer. We often sang. And everything ended in tears. Conversations were remembrances of childhood or about food which our mothers had prepared. We shared recipes, which we made a note of in our head. And there was always the hope of release.

* * * * *

In the summer they began to gather us, the very youngest, for transport. But now few remained. There were barely 100 to choose from. Again we were taken through the Mariinskaia transit camp, where we were joined with other camps, and brought to a transit camp in Krasnoyarsk. We lived there for three months. Again we endured a medical examination, roll call, and various man handlings. We were all recounted and re-examined because no one passed the health examination. They tried to pick out the healthy for Norilsk. The Norilskii region was to the far north and completely uninhabited. There were Arctic nights there – six months of night, six

43

months of day. But none of us were sent there. We again returned to our old master. We returned to Mariinsk for a second year. And again we did not work the whole winter. Such was our story.

Towards spring they began to give us clothing – old felt boots, torn and dirty pea-coats, filthy padded pants. It was clothing from the dead. Everything was so soiled, we cried. Yes, we sobbed when they gave us this clothing. It was terrible to look at, but to wear it on your bare body? But there was no other way. Weak and morally debased, we were led out to prepare the earth under the greenhouse. It was still a long time till it would be warm.

They started to assign us to brigades of 30 people. We were called out by number. When my number was called, I ran. But my felt boots were torn and damp. I slipped and fell and broke my arm. I was sent back to the zone. A splint was put on and I was left. During this fall I severely bumped my head. I vomited. It was clear that I had concussion, but no one paid attention to this. So for a month I wore this splint. Then the doctor, a Georgian, came. He checked me. I still could not wiggle my fingers normally, but he discharged me as healthy.

Again I was sent back to the brigade, but I still could not work. How famished and weak we were! The convoy guards led us far from the zone to a field to pick potatoes. We gathered these frozen potatoes. We made flat cakes without salt, without anything. And we fried them on a sheet of metal on a fire. The soldiers also ate them with us. Not everyone was taken to this work site – some were lucky and happy. We cooked these flat cakes, but we could not just look after ourselves. We tried to share them with those who could not go out to work. But when we approached the guardhouse, they performed a search. If the guards found these flat cakes on someone, then they threw them out. One of the guards, his name was Lemeshko, had many small children. These little urchins grabbed these flat cakes and ran away. Everyone was hungry.

* * * * *

In the spring we were yet again gathered for transport – this time from the Mariinskaia transit camp to the 60th kilometre, to peat, to bog. We were brought to the camp. It was similar to an island, with deep, wide trenches filled with water dug around it. Thugs and criminals had been in the zone before us. They lived there according to their own laws. Before we were supposed to arrive, they had beaten the orderly and killed him. In the barrack there was a puddle of blood. We washed all of this. We scraped it clean with pieces of glass. So we began to make it habitable.

On the next day we began work digging peat. A machine dug and cut it into pieces and we dragged these pieces out of the water, laid them out, and dried them. It was very hard. Everyone was exhausted. Everyone was weak. The majority were ill with night blindness. It was very difficult. We had no communication with our families. We worked there until the weather became too cold. And again we were returned to Novoivanovka, to the Valley of Death. And again everything was the same. There was the same harsh winter. Why was it necessary to torment us so? What was the thought behind this? Even now it's incomprehensible.

* * * * *

We were saved because we were all sentenced under the same article, Article 58, and we were held separately from everyone. It was very good that we were not mixed with common criminals – thieves and rapists. At the transit camp I saw many of our people who had been sentenced to 10 years. Their regime was easier, but not much. For example, they could work at their trade, if it was suitable. Among us Ukrainians, there were tailors and cobblers. They noticed the appalling state we were in and decided to help whoever they could with whatever they could, whenever they saw someone needed something. They repaired shoes for one, a jacket for another, or trousers for another – in a word, they helped us.

In the summer of 1948, we went to work in the greenhouse where tobacco grew. We tended it and gradually tore off leaves, hid the leaves on ourselves, and if we managed to bring it into the zone, then we gathered it all together and gave it to our doctors, who gave it away to the men.

Towards autumn we again were gathered, young, old, and sick, for transport. Again they took us and again we did not know where we were headed. We were brought to Vanino Bay near Vladivostok. We were settled in a transit camp. Tents stood there. And the transit camp was so well maintained, clean paths made from stone, wooden sculptures from tree stumps – it was unbelievable. It seems that Japanese POWs had lived there. After the camps in which we had been in, we stared in wonder at everything there, to see such cleanliness and order, with beds of flowers and even sculptures. All the autumn we lived in this transit camp. Of

45

course, no one told us anything, nor explained. What would happen further with us, we did not know. All we knew was that there was roll call three times a day and very, very meagre food.

* * * * *

1948 – Practically the whole country was behind barbed wire. We, it turns out, were brought to *Berlag*. Still more people had become enemies of the people. Many slaves were needed. The country needed precious metals and wanted to get it without spending any money. For a mere ladle of broth and a ration of bread they had labourers. Stalin gave authority over the prisoners to Beria – and so the *Berlag* was born. Kolyma, Norilsk, Kamchatka, Chukotka, Komi USSR, and all of Siberia were white spots. People perished from the hard work, hunger, cold, and unsanitary conditions. New enemies of the people were found and the dead were replenished with the living. Beria tightened the regime even more. Prisoners were completely undefended. The state decided to move all political prisoners farther from the world, from outside eyes. And all of the young people, and us from the Mariinskaia camp, and all of Siberia began to be taken away by transport. The transports were very large, full of both men and women, if you could call them people. Transport was a horrible ordeal, such persecution – the soldiers with their bayonets and dogs, the roll calls, the taunting.

Suddenly, at the end of October, we were given clothes. Everything was new – pea-coats, padded cotton pants, underwear, felt boots, hat with ear flaps, padded cotton mittens. How glad we were! Everything was new. We had not worn nor seen anything like it for so many years.

On October 25th we were loaded onto the ship *Nogin*. It was dark in the holds, damp and dirty. There were bunks everywhere. We were transported in worse conditions than cattle. The sea at this time of the year was stormy. Everyone vomited. Everyone was sick. No one could eat. Water seeped into the hold up to our knees. We lay side-by-side on the high bunks tightly pressed against each other. Many did not live to reach their assigned place. Our saving grace was prayer. We did not part with prayer. On the 12th day we arrived and found out that we were in Kolyma, in Nagayevo Bay. It was November 7th – a holiday. The country celebrated. We were kept in the holds. On November 9th they began to unload us. The ship had been completely filled; they had sent practically everyone sentenced under Article 58.

Awaiting us were camp bosses and soldiers with dogs. There were tables with our records. Everyone was terribly exhausted, only half alive, most of all the women. There was a deep freeze, wind and snow. The transport was so large that it was impossible to unload everyone in one day. We were counted and led in groups on foot for sanitary processing, and then to a transit camp. We were always called in order, then counted again and again, then sanitary processing. Our clothes were steamed for a sanitary processing treatment. Among the Article 58ers, there were not only those of us assigned to hard labour, but also those assigned to corrective-labour camps, who had 10 year sentences. It is horrible to recall the humiliation that we had to endure, while men, with medals on their shoulder straps, stood looking at us, naked, like things, in order to determine if we were suitable or unsuitable.

Then we went on foot to the Fourth Kilometre camp. We walked. We fell. We were driven on. We reached the camp at night. Again we were counted in the barrack. In the morning, reveille. We were re-counted. Those of us assigned to hard labour were sorted out and put in a special, new barrack with a high fence – a second zone within the main controlling zone. The bunks were damp. There was no floor, just frozen ground. There were stoves made from barrels with diesel, and a special barrel for our needs. The barrack was on a large hill. They brought us food to eat and took it all away when we were done. Everyone slept on the upper bunks, huddling close to each other so as not to freeze. A sheet was all that covered us. We were kept that way until spring.

At the end of May they began to deliver us to the camps along the *trassa*, the road leading off into the interior. Those of us doing hard labour were sent to Butugichag to the camp Vakhanka. Only those doing hard labour were kept there. It was an enormous camp with people of various ages, but in general they were not very old. The camp was a strict regime camp, a uranium mine. We all wore numbers. We were all the same, all grey. Our group, because we were sentenced to hard labour, was one of the last. In 1948 the hard labour sentences were eliminated and people were sentenced to corrective labour camps instead, but still for 25 years, plus five years loss of political and civil rights, and five years exile. There were many of my fellow countrymen there. Numbers were slapped on us and we were no longer people. We were letters and some numbers. My number was M-323. I met girls who had been brought there back in 1945. Many different kinds of people were there – academics of various disciplines, simple workers, nuns and priests. There were many foreigners. How ragged, hungry, and worn out we all were!

There was an ore concentration factory at Vakhanka. Here they jigged tin. Butugichag – these were uranium mine hills. Women worked in these mines. They sent the stones with ore down in little wagons to the crushing station. A narrow-gauge railway had been built and the ore was delivered in little wagons to Vakhanka. Then it was again sent down to another crushing station, which processed it into smaller stones. All this was pulverised into sand and then mixed with water, and then the sand with water fell onto tables. Women did all this. It was the most difficult work, especially at the crushing station. The din, the dust! You do not see one another or hear one another. We were sent to different jobs, mostly in ore processing, but also to cut timber and to the electric power station for firewood, and to do many other jobs. Women did it all.

* * * * *

The head of the camp comes to 'look over the goods.' He asks if there are any complaints, how they are feeding us.

Most reply: "Good, boss."

But I go and say: "It's bad. What they give us is rotting and stinky."

He begins to write and then they leave.

Suddenly, the duty officer comes and summons me to the front of the ranks. And I am given three days and nights in the internal camp prison for what I said.

Locked in this cold, damp cell, I catch a cold. I get a fever and am sent to the hospital. While I am there my group are sent to cut timber.

* * * * *

Here it is true what they say – that fortune is born out of misfortune. My illness turned out to be fortunate. Ore processing was nothing compared to logging. The hospital saved me from that.

But I did not lie in the hospital for long. They checked me the whole time. I was discharged and initially sent to do light work – to carry water. There were two of us. A lot of water was needed. Carry, heat, cut firewood. Then for the winter I was sent to this same factory where the metal is separated from the sand. There were five of us. We were supposed to jig 4 pounds of metal from sand of barren rock. I often was sick. The girls felt sorry for me and supported me. I remember everything. I will be grateful to them my whole life. I remember.

It was not easy there with the icy water and dampness, but nevertheless it was inside and there was heat from the steam. But when there wasn't enough firewood and the factory was unheated, no one thought about us. Damp and wet, they'd order us: "Get dressed and into the vehicle and into the forest for firewood." The temperature often hit minus 50 degrees Celsius. We would be freezing and we would pray. We'd pray that it would be minus 53 degrees Celsius on the thermometer. Then the day would be cancelled. The supervisor would also be freezing along with us. He'd measure the temperature. And we wouldn't be taken out to work.

* * * * *

The ore processing factory was in a big open space, partitioned off with barbed wire, with watchtowers all around, and convoy guards. Our group numbers were summoned to leave the zone. Everyone would stand in formation, in lines of five. The convoy guard would take a roll call and then say 'the prayer' – "Brigade, form up, arms back, head down. A step to the left, a step to the right, we shoot without warning." We were afraid to sneeze. After every two rows there was a guard with a bayonet and a dog. We walked. My nose would be running, but I was afraid to move my hand. They saw everything and if they saw something, then they would immediately command, "Lie down!" They could order us to lie down in the swamp or the mud. If we didn't manage to lie down, they shot and killed us.

* * * * *

In the zone reveille was at 6am. The duty officer would come. We queued up to go to the mess hall; we queued up coming back from the mess hall. We queued up all day long. Someone was not counted? Get up and go outside, queue up. In the winter we froze. After all, we had slept in our damp pants. They got us up often, sometimes several times in one night. Or they got it into their heads to check our cases against the records. They would lead us out at night in the cold, even if there was a blizzard, together with our things. And the soldiers would begin to rip up the boards on the

49

bunks and on the floor. They'd perform a search. It was a long procedure as they went through everything. And then they counted us again. And so on the whole night. And then it was morning and we had to go off to work. This inhumane regime was the most oppressing.

We all prayed quietly to ourselves, because it was forbidden to do otherwise. We believed. We hoped. And so the years passed.

There was no rest in the zone, ever. They found work for us all the time. We were made to go to the burnt hill for Japanese stone pine or to cut firewood in the zone. The most awful was when we came back from work, tired and hungry; it was night, and yet the head of the camps would be standing there and would send us back to the hill to find burnt Japanese stone pine from under the snow for firewood. We would carry it into the storehouse, but the free settlers from the village came at night and took it all. In the morning there would be nothing to prepare lunch. The barracks needed to be heated. Again we were chased out at night. Or they would say to the sick, who they had given a sick day: "You work half the day, then be sick."

When the brigades which stockpiled the firewood for the camp didn't fulfil their quota, they were brought in from work, given food, and then sent, damp and wet, into the lock-up. They spent the night there, then they rose, and were herded into the mess hall to eat the 10 ounces of bread they were given, and then marched off on foot to work. It was 10 kilometres. Those who broke the rules found themselves in this brigade. And just what did breaking the rules mean? She said something, someone informed on her, she was sick and did not go to work, or her number was dirty or she didn't manage to sew it back. And off you would go into the brigade of rule-breakers.

* * * * *

Can you imagine? You walk and sleep on the move. We walked and slept. We even dreamed. We looked like sluggish old women, our faces burned by the frost and the wind. Our skin was cracked, worse than an 80-year-old's.
Very often there were blizzards. The roads were covered with great snow drifts. The factory came to a halt then and everyone was sent to clear the snow. The snow was always tightly compacted. We cleared it in small stages. The last woman threw the snow back farther from the road. The road was only opened in the spring. This road went through the mountain pass, Podumai. In the spring the whole camp was driven out to clear the

snow. The road was long. At this time of the year the sun shines strongly. It radiates strong ultraviolet rays. While we walked, we were all blinded. They made glasses for us out of gauze dyed with manganese or greens, but this did not help. We had burns on our eyes, but there was no mercy. The road needed to be opened. Vehicles needed to come and transport the metal.

In the winter, we carried sacks of metal on our shoulders to the hill where the narrow gauge railroad ran – sacks with exactly 110.23 pounds of ore. We walked, clinging to each other, in groups of threes. God forbid, don't damage the sack! Truly this work was beyond our strength, especially for such emaciated people. Everything could have been different. But this was a special regime. Everything was devised for the extermination of people.

It was that way until the death of Stalin. What happened here when his death was announced? The 'patriots' cried: "The Father is no more! What will happen now?" They walked around and sniffed around and reported who said what, who reacted how. Many people were put in lock-up during those days.

* * * * *

After Stalin's death, the regime became a little milder. Our numbers were removed from our clothes. Sliced bread – a lot of bread – appeared on the tables in the mess hall. We were assured that it would be like this from now on. They began to cook better food. We were led by convoy guards, but now without weapons or dogs. Our hands were freed. Most importantly, the head of our camp, Khomutov, was removed. An account was set up for each person. We began to earn some money. A kiosk appeared in the zone. It was possible to buy some provisions. We earned little, of course. And they deducted for food. But twice a year it was possible to send 20 roubles home. I found my parents in exile in the city of Molotov, Permskaia oblast. And I sent them money. How surprised they were! Where did it come from?

No one spoke officially about an amnesty. Free workers, who also worked with us at the factory, told us that we would be freed soon. We hoped.

In 1954 work at the factory began to be cut back. We were taken to Staraia Veselaia in Magadan. From there we were brought in trucks to the brick factory. How many people perished there! How many became invalids! All of Magadan at that time was composed of camps. Guard towers stood all around it.

In the spring of 1955 it was announced that we could go without convoy guards. We were transferred to the auxiliary farm at the 2nd kilometre near Magadan. From there we were sent to Serdiak to cut hay. We worked there the whole summer. We celebrated the New Year in 1956 there. I remember that on New Year's Day there was a thunderstorm and rain. After New Year we were brought again to Magadan. There was a horse stable there. Girls shovelled the waste from the communal houses and took it away on horse and carts to the field.

And now at this time they began to release people. I was released in the month of March, 1956. I remember the fear and confusion we experienced after being released. After 11 years of camps, I no longer knew anything else. I was unaccustomed to everything. I could not imagine how I would live outside the camps. It seemed to me that I did not know anything at all about life. Yes, that is exactly how it was, in fact. I lived with the mark of the camps on me and nothing more, as if there had been no life before that.

When the official, who gave out documents, asked me where I was going, I began to cry and said that I did not know. He offered me a job in his home, with his family, as a nanny for his young child. His wife had to go out to work. I agreed. They lived at 22 Lenin Street in a communal apartment. I slept in the kitchen. But I was lucky. They were wonderful people – Pavel Pavelovich Popov and Polina Ivanovna. The daughter, Tamara, was one month old. In the beginning I was afraid, but I adjusted and managed. They treated me well, and I respected them. Pavel Pavelovich suggested that I continue my studies. I went to evening school. Later a kind acquaintance helped to fix me up with a job as a medical orderly in the ambulance team. It was difficult then to find work, especially for those of us who had sat in prison.

At this time a one-year nursing course opened. I went to study further. Later I finished a two-year program. I was moved to a nursing position. Later I was sent for a residency in the Oblast Hospital and then worked as a doctor's assistant. And then for 30 years I worked on the ambulance squad. When I retired, I lived on the pension I got from there.

* * * * *

My husband also served time here in the Magadan camps. We met after we had already been released. We married and lived very well. Of course, the camps told on his character and on his nerves. But we got along. He was a very thoughtful husband. He always felt sorry for me and helped. He worked at the bread factory, first as an electrician then as a mechanic.

We had a child, a son. We lived for a long time in a barrack in a small room, nine square metres in size. We were very poor. For a whole year after our son was born, we took care of him in turn. Then with the help of good people, I enrolled my son in a day care centre. It was very difficult to do this then. I remember how my son could not wait for my day off. I also remember how coming home from day care, he pretended to turn on the tap and sputter as if water was running. How he wanted water to come from these taps, but there was no water. We had to carry in water, along with firewood to stoke the stove, in order to wash. It was very hard.

Later we were given a room at 8 Gorky Street. We lived there for 15 years. Our son, Volodia, left for the army from there. And then we were given this apartment in which I live now. My son returned from the army to be with us, but four months later his father passed away. He was 52 years old. And so I remained alone with Volodia. Within a year he married. My son is from God. I have never heard a rude word from him. He has never offended me, never!

* * * * *

In our family there was a strong religious upbringing. All of my family were deep believers from time immemorial, from our grandfathers and great-grandfathers. I remember how my grandmother prayed, and how strictly she observed all the fasts. She knew all her prayers by heart. When we were little, she put us on our knees to pray together with the grown-ups. We had to repeat all our prayers with them. We all observed the commandments. Grandmother read the Holy Bible to us and taught us. Both Father and Mother and we children were all raised in the faith. I believe that only prayers helped me to stand my ground when I ended up in the camps. I survived for this reason alone – because I preserved my faith!

How we prayed in the cells during the interrogations! In camp it was strictly forbidden. You could only say prayers to yourself, inside yourself. Well, when we were held there in Novoivanovka, there we were completely isolated from the world. When it was Sunday, we prayed. We performed the Sunday liturgy. There were also Russians with us there, who, on the whole, were non-believers. They did not participate, but they liked to watch and listen as we sang and prayed.

When we were brought here to Vakhanka, we prayed in our hearts under the blanket and on the road to work. We were walking and we were praying. Of course, prayer saved us. I firmly believe this. And I thank the Lord that he heard our prayers. There was a time in camp when it seemed that it was impossible just to survive. I would address the Lord in such despair! And help always came. We found people who helped in times of trouble, with what little they could. Their support was lifesaving. We obtained help through prayer. We were saved only through prayer. And now I am still saved through my prayers.

We are victims of a communist regime. I never wished anyone evil. Even now I do not know whom I should forgive. Lord, I am thankful for my faith which helped me to survive this.

Andrei Vasilievich Kravtsiv

Born:	August 28th 1928
Where:	Ternavka, Skalevskii region, Lvivskaia oblast
Country:	Ukraine
Arrested:	1945
Sentence:	10 years corrective labour camps, plus 5 years loss of rights
Released:	November 1955
Rehabilitated:	March 25th 2004, Certificate No. 0189365

I WAS BORN ON AUGUST 28th 1928 in a beautiful village in the Lviv oblast in the Carpathian Mountains – the ever-green Carpathians. Our family had many children – eight brothers and one sister. We had a large farm, very large, somewhere around 250 acres of land. We worked it ourselves. Everyone worked on this land.

In our family, we had our own beautiful, vocal ensemble. Our oldest brother had completed his studies at the Lviv Conservatory. Almost all the boys had had at least a basic musical education. They played folk instruments – the guitar, the *domra*, the mandolin and the *balalaika*. I finished seven years in a general education school. During my childhood, I participated in the church choir. I sang in church. Then I entered the Lviv music school. But I did not finish as I was arrested in my third year.

It happened like this. We students in the school had formed a literary union called '*Prosvita*' and studied the works of Lesa Ukrainka, Ivan Franko, Taras Shevchenko, Aleksandr Pushkin, Yuri Lermontov and other classics. We also studied the history of Ukraine from the book by Krushevski, who was the first president of Ukraine, after an independent Ukraine was declared in 1918. Krushevski was a historian and so also wrote the history of Ukraine. This book was forbidden, but we studied it anyway.

One student informed on us. One night NKVD workers appeared and conducted a search of the school. They found the history of Ukraine by Krushevski under my pillow. They arrested me and a whole group of classmates.

I was sentenced first in Lviv. During the interrogations, I was severely beaten. The investigators particularly liked to interrogate us at night. The cries and moans of women could be heard throughout the whole prison.

At the trial I renounced my testimony. I said that I had been severely beaten and was forced to sign a statement regarding things that I had not done. I was returned to the cell again. Of course, after this, they tried to severely intimidate me using torture. They thrust needles under my fingernails and smashed my fingers in the door, with these needles still under my fingernails.

Then a *troika* sentenced me. This was a military tribunal. They did not ask me any questions there. I was not even allowed to make a final statement – nothing. I was given 10 years in a correctional labour camp for belonging to an organisation of Ukrainian nationalists. And so began my life in transport to Magadan.

* * * * *

My sentence was handed down in 1945. But since I was 17 years old, I was considered a juvenile. All of us young prisoners were separated. We remained in a transit camp in Lviv. For almost a year we worked restoring a factory in the city of Sknilov, near the airport. We carried out various building jobs. Then in 1946, we were taken to Donbas, to the city of Stalino (now Donetsk).

There we restored a completely damaged factory. In the autumn of 1946, we were taken from Stalino to Estonia. First, we were held in a camp in Narva. There was some kind of former military barracks there. We dismantled the Leonovetskaia Fortress, where Peter the Great, in his time, had fought with the Swedes. And then all the young prisoners were taken away and brought to the Gulf of Finland. Some large deposits of precious minerals had been found there. We built some kind of factory.

In the beginning, that is for about the first six months, we were taught construction work – plastering, painting, finishing, how to make capitals and cornices. And then we worked on the factory. In the autumn of 1948, we were taken from there and sent by transport to the city of Taishet in the Irkutsk oblast. Japanese prisoners of war had been there. They had just been released at that time, although many had remained. They were afraid to leave, knowing what kind of reception awaited them at home.

We built the Taishet highway. And there was this slogan: "On the highway, there is no rain." This meant that we worked in any weather, in any conditions. The midges and mosquitoes fed on us terribly. It was simply impossible to bear them. The living conditions were austere. We worked there about a year. And in 1950 we were sent by transport to Magadan.

We travelled in cattle trucks for more than a month. Then we ended up in a transit camp at Vanino Port. This transit camp is always recalled with horror, and not just by me. There is a famous song about it, called *Vanino Port*.

After that we sailed for five days by ship to Magadan. We were unloaded in Nagayevo Bay and sent to a transit point at the 4th Kilometre. We were quarantined.

Everyone was very afraid of Butugichag – a mine where uranium was extracted. I ended up in Butugichag. Although, you could say that I was lucky – I did not work in the mine itself. I was assigned to work at the ore concentration plant, where the uranium ore was purified. We gave to the so-called *kum* – the godfather – who was a security officer in the office of safety, our signed pledge that we would not divulge state secrets. When you worked in one section, you were not supposed to know what was being done in another. But, of course, we knew, since we talked among ourselves.

And then in 1953, I was put under the command of the camp administration, because I had learned construction skills. We repaired offices in the bureau. On one of those days we were working as usual and heard on the radio, which hung in the corridor, that Stalin had died. We were immediately sent back to the camp with a convoy of guards. There were three of us. We had just gone through the guardhouse and entered the zone and – I don't know why this happened to me – I began to shout: "Stalin kicked the bucket! Stalin kicked the bucket!" The prisoners who were outside began to shout! "Hurrah! Hurrah!"

I was immediately sent to the isolation cell, to the lock-up. I was quickly sentenced a second time. I was given six more years.

* * * * *

We were located in camps. There was no communication – just the zone and the convoy. It seemed like complete isolation. But following the death of Stalin, strikes began to take place throughout all of the camps in the Soviet Union – not for political reasons, but with demands that the bars on the windows be removed, that our numbers, which we wore on our clothes, on the back, chest, pants and hat, be removed, that the barracks not be locked at night, that the *parasha*, the chamber pot, be taken out of the barracks, that the 12 hour work day be eliminated and made just a 10 hour work day.

When I was sentenced and given another six years, I was brought to Ust-Omchug for a trial. But after Stalin's death there was an amnesty. And right there in the court, half of my sentence was knocked off – just three years remained.

Soon after this we were taken away from Butugichag. The ore there had a low uranium content. At that time, somewhere in the near East, ore was discovered that had a high uranium content. The Soviet Union concluded an agreement for the ore with the higher content. Butugichag was closed.

Stepan Mudrii and I ended up at the mine called Belov. This was also in the Tenkinskii region. We worked there in a gold mine. We extracted ore. Again, I was lucky that, after Stalin's death, the camp climate changed. We were no longer restricted to a ration of just 23 ounces of bread; instead bread was placed on the table — take as much as you pleased. We did not even finish all the bread that we were given. The bars were removed from the windows. Some kind of air vent appeared at last. We were allowed to wear our hair up to three centimetres long. The numbers on our clothes were removed.

* * * * *

I organised a choir at the mine. Stepan Mudrii also sang in it. He is in a photograph that I have. All the young men who participated in the chorus tried to transfer to work on one shift so that it was possible to practice. I practiced with each one separately, whenever anyone had some time. And then I brought them all together and we practiced as a group.

60

Many youths were sent embroidered shirts from their families at home. Some boots made from leatherette were found in the camp. In our camp the leader of the Culture and Education Unit was very good. He was from eastern Ukraine. He attended every practice. He treated this very seriously. True, he checked every text, every word to make sure that there was not anything seditious there.

In camp there were many good musicians from Russia and Ukraine, from Hungary and Estonia – for example, Udo Mesner. He gave me extra music lessons. And twice a week I gave him 10.5 ounces of bread from my ration. He was an accomplished accordionist. There was a priest, Onufrii Ivanovich Ivaniuk, a man with a conservatory education from Lviv. On the whole, so many of the most capable and educated people were in prison camps! And so many of these did not survive!

A good club was built in the village at the Belov Mine. There was a good stage and even an orchestra pit. During the day this was used as a mess hall, and in the evening as a club.

I remember one evening that we performed in honour of the annual anniversary of the Great October Socialist Revolution. All the workers of the village and mine – men, women, military and civilian – came to the concert. It was a packed hall. The singers were all young and handsome. They had recuperated a little bit somehow, after the loosening up of the regime which occurred following the death of Stalin. They looked so wonderful – everyone in his embroidered shirt.

When the curtain opened, all the women in the hall sighed. True, we only sang one song. I aimed to produce a very good sound. There was one musician from Estonia, a violinist. Everyone sang accompanied by the orchestra, a rather original ensemble. But mostly they sang *a capella*. They loved singing *a capella* more than anything.

One song which we had prepared we were forbidden to sing at the concert. I don't even remember why! There wasn't anything particular about it. It was the Ukrainian song 'Wide Meadows, Green Forest'. We kept this song in reserve and did not plan to sing it. But the applause, the applause in the hall! I walked out of the wings and said: "We will sing 'Wide Meadows.'" We sang only one couplet. The security officer ran out on the stage. Immediately they closed the curtain. It was forbidden to sing it. They forbade it. Right away I was sent to the isolation cell. And the singers were sent back to work. That's how the concert concluded!

* * * * *

In 1955 when I had finished the 10 years of my primary sentence, according to Article 54.11, betrayal of the motherland, and Point 1, participation in a Ukrainian nationalist organisation, I still had three years of the second sentence. Having served out my first sentence, I was now permitted to go without a convoy guard. I was sent to cut lumber in the same Tenkinskii region, in the village of Kula. I didn't work there for long.

* * * * *

We had a brigade of 18 people. On one of the days, according to the schedule, I worked as the cook. As usual, everyone came to eat supper. And the head of the Cultural-Educational Unit came. He greeted me. Of course, he remembered me well as I had worked for several years at the Belov Mine and had put on many artistic performances there, which he had supervised it.

They begin to eat and he is offered what has been prepared. He asks: "Who prepared this?"

I answer: "I, Citizen Boss."

"Well, this is the last time you will cook," he says, "and the last time you will eat here."

"But why? Did something happen?"

"I am not Citizen Boss to you. I am Comrade. Your release came."

I say: "Citizen Boss, you're not joking, are you? Because such a joke could break one's heart."

"No, I am not joking. Here," he says, "sign."

It was 1955, the month of November. I had served just a half year of my second sentence and that was it. At night the young men began to alter my clothes – one worked on my pants, another on a shirt, another on boots and another on my pea-coat in order to smarten up my clothing at least a little bit. They gave me something new. And that was it. The next day I was out the gate.

* * * * *

I went to Ust-Omchug. I was given a passport. Then I went to Magadan. They stopped at a transit point, just before Dukcha. I was given some money, some miserly *kopecks* for my work. And I remained here in Magadan.

During the first period after being released from camp, I very much wanted to leave for home back in Ukraine. But I could not, because I had been deprived of my civil and political rights. For five years I could not leave. The same was true for my youngest brother, who was in Kazakhstan. When he was released, he was taken by convoy to Boguchana, Krasnoyarsk region. He also did not have the right to leave for five years. He married there. I had a similar situation. Since I was forbidden to leave, I decided to stay and work.

During these years I lost everything dear to me, all of my family. All this communist ideology destroyed everything. Take 1933: in Ukraine around 9 million people died from famine – that is what the statistics say. The young had to leave in order to survive. And when a delegation from Ukraine went to Stalin to request help, he supposedly was surprised. "What? There is a famine in Ukraine? That cannot be."

At the time of my release, a revue of artistic performances was to take place in Magadan. Many of my acquaintances from camp were there. They asked me to help with arranging the performances at the sewing factory. In one of the dormitories, the girls had gathered and organised a vocal ensemble. The majority were former prisoners from the Ukraine. I joined in with them on the closing night of the performances. We received a first class diploma.

My life began after my release. I went to study at an evening school for young workers. I worked and studied. I finished the eleventh grade. And since I had proven myself with this women's ensemble, the City Committee of the Trade Unions sent me to work in Novaia Vesyolaia as the club manager. I agreed.

My working salary was miserly, like that of all culture workers, teachers and media professionals. I wanted to dress up, and yes, I needed something to live on. I did not work there long, perhaps half a year. The City Committee of Trade Unions recommended me for study in the city of Leningrad. I was transferred to the House of Culture for Auto Transportation Workers. I worked there for 30 years. I finished my studies at the Higher Professional Union School named Krupskaia.

In my labour book there are two remarks – "Accepted" and "Released." That's all.

* * * * *

In 1960 I married. I have a good family, two sons and a daughter. I had the kind of work that took up all my time. I loved this work very much. I gave it my whole soul. On the whole it was evening work – performance clubs. I worked closely with the schools. We had about 500 children who studied daily in various groups, but this helped to keep the kids off the streets. They had something to occupy themselves with.

One of my sons finished Moscow State University. He found work there and married. He works as a general director of a joint enterprise with Japan. My second son works here in Magadan as a lawyer in a bank. My daughter qualified from the Magadan Teaching Institute. She lives in Magadan and teaches English and Russian.

In 1990 we decided to go with the family to our homeland, to Ukraine, to settle a question about an apartment, and then live there for good. In the Carpathian Mountains, where our home was before, everything had been confiscated because my father was also arrested in 1946 for not giving 40 pounds of grain. He gave two tons, but was short those 40 pounds. They arrested him and sentenced him to six years in prison. He died in a mine in Donbas.

My younger brother and my sister were also arrested. Shurina was arrested and her five small children, who were aged between three and 10 years old at the time, were left without a mother. No one cared that her children were left alone.

Who was left from this big family? I alone remained. No one else was left. I thank God for my survival. All of my brothers died between 20 and 22 years of age. Two died in the war. My oldest brother, like other prisoners at that time, was executed in prison in 1941 when the Germans attacked.

I arrived in Ukraine with my family and built a house there. I built it almost all by myself. I built a good home. I was the architect for the house. Then they asked me to organise a church choir there in our village. It was a large choir with 50 men and women and we sang in four-part harmony. They told me that they would help me build my house, if only I would work with the choir. I agreed. I worked with them about a year and a half. They sang for the Church.

In Ukraine, we have the Ukrainian Catholic church. The worship and liturgy are in Ukrainian. My students were working people. I was able to work individually with each one. "Vania, today I have time, come by." And then: "Natasha, come when you can." I practised with the altos and the sopranos separately and then brought them together; then the tenors and basses, first by themselves and then together. Without a leader, they all sang independently. On their own, they sang in two parts as best they could. It is easier, of course, to teach people from scratch rather than to teach in this situation, where they were used to singing one way for years, and then needed to be re-taught. But I reached, perhaps not completely, but near to, professional level. It was one of the best choirs in the region.

* * * * *

My family did not return to Ukraine. It was difficult to find work there. Before I was arrested, they had to beg people there to go to work on the railroad, even as a railway engineer; now you had to pay a huge bribe just to get fixed up with a job there. Of course, this was not official.

In 2002 my son came. He travelled with his family on vacation and he sad: "Papa, come to Magadan. We can't come to Ukraine. And you are here alone. People still think that we abandoned you and went to Magadan."

I left Ukraine and I regret it very much. When I left, the choir members cried at the last Mass and asked me not to go. But…

* * * * *

I arrived back in Magadan. At first I felt worse here. In the Carpathians the air is clean. There is a forest with pine, beech, and spruce. There are beautiful mountains. Nearby, about seven kilometres from us, are large tourist resorts. There are roads into the mountains. Many tourists travel there, especially in the winter, on pilgrimages.

I came here to Magadan. My wife was born here. Her parents were from Ukraine; from Nikopolia, Dnepropetrovsk oblast. In 1937 they were brought here. She was born here. She is the daughter of repressed parents. So we lived.

Life follows its own course. My children have already grown up. They have their own families. And I am still strongly drawn to Ukraine. So I will probably go, but maybe not for good.

* * * * *

The religious upbringing that I received in my childhood helped me a great deal in the camps. We prayed, although if caught we were put in the lock-up. The majority of those who prayed were Ukrainians, but there were also Latvians and Estonians. We were believers, but the locals, the Russians, were not.

In the camps, the camp administration specially planted their own *seksot*, as they called them – stool pigeons, particularly those who had not been sentenced under political articles, but under criminal articles – thieves and repeat offenders. They informed on everyone. They were connected to security officers and informed the 'godfather'. The other prisoners, of course, fought back in their own way if they found out who was the informant. They would put him through a 'dark night'. They put a sack over his head and then beat him almost to death. They also meted out retribution.

I am sure that prayer helped us and helped us to stand our ground. Imagine Butugichag, the uranium mine. Before us there were prisoners of war there, about 3,000 Polish officers. They worked there and almost all perished there. Then almost the same number of hard labourers was brought there. Hard labourers were the people who had been sentenced to 15 years or more. On the whole they were all from western Ukraine. Out of these young people, almost no one, especially the drillers, came out alive.

We breathed this same air. We drank this same water. A stream went through there. And I do not know how I was saved. Evidently, God himself helped me. I prayed a lot. When I prayed, I always asked and promised that if I just survived, if I was released and able to return to my homeland, then I would buy something special and make my own sacrifice for the Church. And I promised to buy a copy of the Holy Gospels.

66

In 1960 I went on vacation back to my homeland for the first time since my arrest. I arrived, but at that time I could not find a copy of the Gospels anywhere. Soviet ideology did not allow people to believe in God, only in the Communist Party. Yes, even the church was closed. At one time they wanted to put a museum in the church. But somehow people saved it, defended it, and guarded it at night.

Only in 1991, in Lviv, did I buy what I wanted. The Book of the Gospels is very beautiful, decorated with gold. It was very expensive. These are the Holy Gospels that I bring to church. And on one of the feast days, the priests blessed it very solemnly. When I did this, everything became somehow easier. I had fulfilled what I had promised; I had done my duty.

Here in Magadan in the community with Fr Michael, the pastor of our parish, the Nativity of Christ, I have received a great deal much – a kind of spiritual charge, a kind of fulfilment. Yes, I receive so much; I am very satisfied. God, give Fr Michael health and strength! Fr. Michael gives himself completely to his calling. He treats each person who comes with the utmost attention, with a kind word – especially the elderly and children.

I go to church and I feel better. It is good for me now. My soul is at rest. I pray and life becomes easier. Prayers can create miracles for us.

I know this for certain.

Stepan Prokopovich Mudrii

Born: September 16th 1931
Where: Ternavka, Zhidachevskii
region, Drohobych Oblast
Country: Ukraine
Arrested: 1950
Sentence: 25 years hard labour,
plus 5 years loss of civil
and political rights
Released: 1958
Rehabilitated: 1992

MY FRIEND AND I HAD JUST ARRIVED HOME FROM A TRIP. They were ready waiting for us. The two of us were arrested together in our native village. A scarf was thrown over my head and I was bundled into the car. Three people were already laying there.

The scarf was only removed when we were brought into the holding cell. Through a small window I saw the others who shared in this misfortune. But I did not manage to see everyone. The NKVD workers tortured us for six months. They beat us horribly.

It was very frightening during the first days. They demanded that I admit to everything and give them the names of other people. I was tortured, I was severely tortured. The main thing was that when I was being tortured myself, a woman or girl on the other side of the wall was also being tortured. It was impossible to listen to those shouts. It was awful. I didn't have the strength to endure it.

They beat me and beat me, coming at me from one side. I would double over to evade the blows and they would hit me in the solar plexus. That was it. Then they would pour a bucket of water over me and carry me out. They had beaten me everywhere. The torture was terrifying.

Then I was brought to an administrative centre in Drohobych. Here we were sentenced. This happened in 1950. I was given a sentence of 25 years, plus five years loss of civil and political rights. Three of our comrades were executed.

* * * * *

After this my 'adventure' through the transit camps began. In Lviv we were loaded onto freight carriages and sent to Vanino Bay.

We travelled for probably one and a half months. When we saw the sea at Vanino, we knew the road that lay ahead of us was to Magadan. Anyone who had some kind of clothing bartered everything, everything that they could. I had two shirts and a good suit. They were sent to me in prison, because I had nothing with me when I was arrested.

We were there in Vanino for about two weeks. Then we were sent to Magadan. 10,000 people were brought on that one ship. There were all kinds of young people. It was very difficult. Some even tried to escape, but no one was successful.

We were brought to Magadan and unloaded in the seaport of Nagayevo. We were sent on foot to Transportnaia Street, where there was a sanitary processing station. People were put under hot water – they put it on full blast so that several people collapsed in a dead faint.

After this we were settled at the Fifth Kilometre mark from the city, on the right hand side. We were kept there for, I think, three weeks – not long. The 'merchants' – camp supervisors – arrived from the mines. The very youngest, those who were most capable of work, were chosen. Then the merchants loaded us into vehicles and took us off. There were five rows of five, a total of 25 people, in the truck.

We did not know where we were being taken. We were brought to Butugichag, to the uranium mines. I ended up in Katsegan. There was this camp there on the hill, Katsegan. After a few days we were sent to the mine. I worked for nearly three years in this mine at first as an assistant, later as a driller.

Once I was assigned two girls as trainees – one was from Latvia, the other was from Ukraine. I had to teach them to work with the miner's pick. I could not imagine how to teach these poor girls to work with this piece of iron. I said: "You don't have to. I will do it all myself." I remember the surname of the Latvian girl – Dzhidra. She, poor thing, became quite attached to me. She worried that she could not do anything with this pick. I told her more than once: "Well, dear, don't worry. Everything will be fine."

Soon after, I needed an operation to remove my appendix. The girls asked the supervisor to let them visit me: "Allow us to go to Styopa's tent."

By the way, a German performed the operation on me. The cut was not that big. The operation too, took literally nine minutes. They took me off the anaesthetic. "That's it," they told me. "You are free to go."

But of course I couldn't "go". I was not "free". The medic Sasha took me by the arm to my tent. I was kept there for two weeks and then sent back to work.

* * * * *

So many different people were in the camps – scholars, professors, engineers. Some people were very educated, cultured and from such well-to-do families. But camp life, as they say, shattered the fates of many. Such is our life. Everything passed like a dream… like a dream.

* * * * *

In the camp, people sentenced under various articles, both political (Article 58) and criminal, were all accommodated together, all pell-mell. A skirmish took place among us. As a solution to the incident, we – probably 30 of us – were swiftly despatched to Yakutsk. We were assigned to gold mines, which were located 200 kilometres past Ust-Nera. I worked there more than two years.

While I was working in the mine, there was a cave-in. I was pulled out with two broken ribs. I lay in the infirmary. I healed a little. I was taken to work in an open-pit mine. In order to let me heal properly, I was transferred from the mine to the surface. But I did just the same work there, only on the surface rather than underground.

* * * * *

After Stalin died, our numbers were removed – we had until then had prisoner numbers on our clothing, on our head, on our chest. The regime became a little easier. More bread appeared on the tables. They began to count our work days. We earned money. Now it was possible to go to the buffet and order something edible.

During my incarceration, we were, as they say, "thrown about" the camps many times. We were brought back from Ust-Nera to Tenkinski region, Magadanskaia Oblast. Here Andrei Kravstiv and I met after Butugichag. We met at the Mine called Belov. We worked there at the factory. I worked there on scrubbing instruments. I panned gold-bearing sand. I extracted gold.

And I was released from there in 1958, I think. We were awaiting a commission that went around the camps and handled case reviews and the release of prisoners. Many of us were released then. We were told that we could go wherever we wanted. We were each given a 100 roubles or something around that for the trip, so that we could get where we wanted to go. We wanted to go home to Ukraine, where each of us had lived before this. But I wasn't able to leave for there right away. I was completely without clothes, and penniless. I decided to work a little. I met an acquaintance who had been freed a year earlier. He worked at the seaport. He arranged for me to work with them until the end of the navigation season.

Aleksander Nikitovich Shevchenko was the head of the port back then. It was clear that he liked me and we talked. I began to work; but when the last ships of the season were sent out, I went to him and said: "I am going, Aleksander Nikitovich..."

He asked: "Styopa, where will you go? Stay here and work for me." Well, he offered me a contract. I signed. I stayed for a year, then a second, and so on. Then children came.

* * * * *

My wife and I had met here in Magadan. She too had served her sentence and she was also from Ukraine –from Lviv. She worked at the sewing factory after her release. She had been released earlier than me – I think in 1955.

It was hard to make a home. We had children. We took in my wife's mother, who was also from Ukraine. She too had been sentenced. She served out her time in Norilsk. And I brought my sister, Vera, here from Ukraine.

And then I fell seriously ill. An ambulance took me straight from work. The doctors began to investigate. It turns out it was a recurrence of an illness that I had earned in the uranium mines. My lungs were in a terrible state, because of the dust. They did not work as they should at all. I lay in the hospital for about a year. I was given invalid status.

* * * * *

When I remember the years of my life following my release, I find I can say many good things about Magadan. The people who had served time here understood everything. We supported each other. We were responsible, conscientious. Many of us are no longer alive now; many left. I renew old acquaintances with them when I am in Ukraine.

The first time I went to Ukraine, the local officials did not want to register me. I wanted to be registered in my homeland. I tried everywhere, and I was refused everywhere. They would look in my passport, see that this person had been in Magadan against his own free will, and they would refuse. The first time was some time in 1969, when I went to bury my father.

Two years passed and my mother died, but I could not go back then. I had only just arrived back from there and I had no money. So I did not even go to the funeral. It was later when I had saved a little money that I went on holiday, and then I visited her grave.

I still have a sister and a brother there in Ukraine.

But since my release, I have lived in Magadan. My wife and I almost lived to see our golden wedding anniversary. We only had to hold out just a little longer, but she died. First my daughter died, and then within two years my wife died. Now only my two sons remain. One lives in Magadan, the other on the mainland in Pskov. I have seven grandchildren. That is our family.

* * * * *

It is, of course, difficult to remember my past in the camps. The humiliations of those sentenced were awful – moral debasement, hunger, excessive work. The main thing was these jobs. They taunted us so much that if someone was not liked, that person was sent to get something from outside the fenced-off zone. It didn't matter what. The person just approached the forbidden zone and he was shot with an automatic weapon by the guard in the tower. It was frightening.

We were brought out to work when it was minus 50 degrees Celsius. At 8am we were led to the mine and at 8pm the convoy guards brought us back to the camp. We worked 12 hour shifts in the mine. We were led there in columns of five. The convoy guards carried automatic weapons and walked with dogs. Then came the roll call, and while the available prisoners were counted, four or five people were carried away.

People died from malnutrition, from the cold. Our clothing was a jersey, a pea-coat. You wore a quilted jacket and felt boots, and that's all. Really, what kind of clothing is that for such freezing cold? My fellow countrymen still managed to hold on. But prisoners from the Baltic countries, and Poles – well, they were not used to this from their old lives, and they fell more often.

Many priests were in the camps, though later the authorities began to clear them out. I sat in camps with many priests, both Catholic and Orthodox.

Faith, in such complicated and trying times, helped us to stand our ground in camp. We never lay down to sleep without praying. In the morning when we rose, we also prayed. We tried to celebrate religious holidays as we could.

Now and then we came upon good supervisors, those who worked in the mines. The supervisor of my shift was Grigorii Ivanovich. He knew when it was Easter and Christmas. His wife prepared him a little something tasty. He would always bring it down the mines in his pocket and say: "This is for you for your holiday." He was not embarrassed to offer us these treats.

Different people treated us in different ways. Over the years we became friendly with many people in the camps. But many of them are no longer alive. Those of us who still live here get together whenever we can; and we talk on the phone. Some have left. Some live in eastern Ukraine, others in Lviv. We still write to each other. I remember everyone, but if memory, as they say, lets me down, then there are the photographs that we took while still in the camps. These pictures conjure up vivid memories of the people who shared my fate. I remember who lived side by side with me during that most arduous time.

There is even a photograph where Andrei Vasilievich Kravtsiv and I were photographed together. He directed a choir and I accompanied them on the mandolin. This was at the Mine with the name of Belov. We even put on a concert. We travelled. And it was there that we were photographed with the camp supervisor. There were all kinds.

* * * * *

I go to pray at the Church of the Nativity of Christ. I feel as though some kind of relief comes to me. I pray there and at home by myself. I have my own prayers for myself, for those who have passed away and for health. They are powerful prayers. I feel how God helps me. I have, you know, this sense. I ask about something and things become completely different for me. It is such a relief when the things I have prayed for are realised. When you live with God, it is easier to live.

The meetings of the repressed which are conducted at the church are absolutely vital. The pastor, Fr. Michael (who is a person who worries and hurts on behalf of his people) has brought everyone together. This is good. It is good because I meet people whom I know, people of my age and my generation. We remember amongst ourselves what happened and then – best of all! – we sing the very best songs. Song after song, we sing! In a difficult moment Ukrainians have always sung songs. We were saved by songs. The holidays come – we remember Christmas carolling and Easter songs. We have not forgotten any of them.

I am in my seventh decade now, and it seems as if it was all just yesterday. Now the main thing is to live, to live to the end quietly and peacefully, so that no one climbs deeper into my soul and worries me. That is what I think.

I have not forgotten my camp number – 964. These numbers were sewn on my jacket. And my jacket is lying around somewhere, preserved.

I kept it. I thought: "I will keep it to remember, so that nothing of what I endured will be forgotten."

Anna Korneevna Portnova

Born:	March 2nd 1924
Where:	Shutromintsy, Ternopilskaia region, Zalishchyky
Country:	Ukraine
Arrested:	March 2nd 1946
Sentence:	15 years hard labour and 5 years loss of civil and political rights
Released:	May 6th 1956
Rehabilitated	

AS LONG AS I CAN REMEMBER, beginning with early childhood, it was so hard for us to live! How very hard! We experienced so many heartaches. We were always half-starved. First under Polish rule, we worked for the 'Pan' – the local noble. Then the Russians came: "Let us organise collective farms." The cows were taken away, then the horses. How did our collective farms begin? From what? Our land became those collective farms. And immediately we were ordered: "Bring your horses, and your cows." How many tears there were!

"I will not give my cow. I won't take it from the children," promises the husband as he leads his horse to the collective farm. His wife cries. "You – go to work on the collective farm, just don't touch the cow."

And my Mama said that we would work on the collective farm, just so long as the cow was not taken. By spring, we had all gone to work on the collective farm. Only the cow remained. Oh, how many tears there were!

* * * * *

Our people were good, hard-working believers. I have somehow only now begun to understand that such honesty, such morals among our people were founded only on the church, on prayer and the Commandments – do

81

not steal, do not kill, do not lie. And also on the Beatitudes – feed the hungry, take the traveller into your home, give drink to the thirsty. All of this was instilled in us from birth. You were born and your mother immediately carried you to church. And she prayed there. I have observed the Muslims, how they bow to the earth with their head. We also bowed the same way. We also knew that without God there is no path, but that with God there is everything. Lord help us, be our helper, come to our help, we prayed – at home, at work, in church, in the field and off the field. Everything is done with God's help. And so, on this morality, everything was held together from generation to generation. It had nothing to do with literacy, but with this purity, this faith.

* * * * *

What we didn't go through when the war began! What a terrible time it was! The front line was right there in Ternopil! Our whole region was destroyed! There was such fear, hunger and grief. It is impossible to think about it even now. How did the women, our mothers, bear all this? And we were just little girls – how did we survive? Like shoots that poke through the asphalt – that is how we made our way through.

In 1945, the arrests started. The Russians became suspicious of everyone and began to accuse everyone. What did we feed people? They wanted to know. Who hid out in our homes? But for us, they were not partisans, just people. Everyone came through the village. The city was surrounded. There were various garrisons with many soldiers. But everyone passed through the country villages – those who escaped the Germans, those who had not joined the army, those who were against this group or that group. We could not distinguish who was who. And who asked us anyway? If you didn't give them something to eat, they would take it by force.

They would come: "Mother, feed us. Mother, feed us." One time Mama did not save anything for us. There were some potatoes in their skins, she gave them all away. Some flat cakes. We almost never saw bread. There was nothing with which to fire the Russian stove. Yes, and there was nothing with which to bake. You bake something, and then give it up. If you put potatoes on to boil, there is a raid! They come for this pot, for shelter and these half-cooked potatoes. It is frightening to remember what we endured.
In 1945 the war began for everyone. It became an even more frightening time for us. Looting took place all around us. Everything became incomprehensible – who was shooting at whom from around the corner.

And then the arrests started. On our street alone, 15 girls were arrested. I watched as one was arrested, then another, and then a third one was gone.

I remember Annushka Lapinskaia. She was born in 1929. She was 15 back then. Some men came to her. They asked for something to eat. Her mother baked some flat cakes, but there was no milk. Since we were all neighbours, we tried to support and help each other in any way we could. And we gave anything to anyone in the hope that they would leave a little quicker. A neighbour gave her some milk for the men. They ate, drank and left.

In the morning other soldiers come and approach that kind neighbour, demanding: "Give us something to eat."

He replies: "Here are the flat cakes that I have, but yesterday I gave our milk to the neighbour's girl."

They shout, "No one was here before us. We just arrived here. We are the first. Where is this girl?"

The neighbour says: "I will not deceive you. She lives across the street."

And they go over there.

"Where is Anna Lapinskaia?"

Her mother says: "This is my daughter."

I am there at their house at that very moment. I see all this for myself.

"Well, get your things. You are coming with us."

Her mother, in tears, says: "Where are you taking a child? She's still just a child."

There is no arguing, no conversation. To insist is useless. In the best case scenario, you receive the butt of gun against your back.

And so the girl was taken. It was never sorted out. She served 10 years, just like me, for nothing at all.

* * * * *

In 1945 the Soviet power structure began to be set up. There was now a director on our collective farm. How we wanted to go out to the fields, to plough, to sow and to plant something, because we had endured such hunger. I was now 22 years old. Our neighbours found some abandoned, lame horse. Maybe the Germans left it. They healed its leg and went and ploughed a little bit of land. And I also went and ploughed a little piece. I don't know how many square feet, but I ploughed it myself. There was just a little grain, which our neighbours gave us. I sowed it with my own hands. I had seen how the old men sowed grain.

Then I noticed how many trees we had cut down in our yard for the war. We needed to plant trees. As a girl, 12 or 13 years old, I often worked in the forest where seedlings were planted. I went and dug up a young apple tree. During this time they had grown. They were already tall, almost as tall as me. I dug up three seedlings at a time. I went and planted them. The second time I dug up another three seedlings. Ten years later after I had been released, Mama wrote to tell me that she had gathered a bucket of apples from my apple trees. Only I planted them too close together. I did not take into consideration how thickly they would grow. So later they were intertwined by the roots, as if they embraced one another. When I came home, I hugged each apple tree, when no one was looking. And the apples on them – some were white, others red.

But I did not see how the apple trees took root, nor how the wheat grew. 1946 started – January, February and March. March 2nd was my birthday. On March 1st Mama said: "I am going to visit Grandmother. You, Anna, go and spend the night at the neighbour's house." I guessed that she wanted to bake me something at my grandmother's house for my birthday, as a surprise.

And in the morning, on my birthday, when I am still sleeping, they come.

"Get your things," they order. "Get your things."

I do not even ask where or why – I have turned to stone.

I already know what awaits me – so many girls have already been taken away!

* * * * *

I was brought to a village not far away. It was obvious from the many soldiers there that it was a garrison. I was led into a room. "Lie down," they

84

ordered, then lifted my skirt and beat me. I do not even know what they beat me with – either a lash or something else, maybe a switch cut from a tree. Even now I cannot watch when they show someone being beaten on television. I cannot. And then they hit me on the head so that I fell under the stove. I only regained consciousness in the morning. Since then I have had reduced hearing. Later I was brought to Chertkiv, to a prison.

In prison the cells were very long and narrow. We slept with a head here, a head there, like herring. Near me lay a girl also from our region. Some kind of water oozed from her buttocks from where she had been assaulted. When the broth was distributed to us to eat, we pleaded with the guards. "Take this girl. Treat her." No! No one! Nothing! She suffered because she too had fed a partisan.

And what if we had not given them something to eat, then what? It would have been the butt of a gun across the head. There were young girls growing up in these homes, so a mother worried about them. Yes, she would give the last flat cake to whoever asked, just so that they eat quickly and go. Everyone went to the villages. Where else could they go? And who did not come? One day someone would come: "I am a Czech." The next day: "I am a Turk." Whom didn't we see? No one wanted to die, no one. I think that even today if someone hides out in your home and demands something to eat, yes, if your child is with you, you would go to a store and buy him everything. A mother would not only give away food, but put her own head on the block for her children.

Well, that was how it was at the interrogations. They did not beat me during the interrogations. They just asked me the same questions day in and day out. One day they asked. The next day they asked it again. And again. And yet another time. I said that yes, we had fed them and yes, we had given them milk. When they assaulted me, I understood that if they needed to, they would beat something out of you, no matter what. And so I answered yes to everything. Everything else I did not see. I do not know. And however they extracted it, the answer was the same: "I do not know. I do not know." But if I said "yes," then already it was clear that I would be sentenced to 10 years.

One day I say: "Well, comrade, I already told you that I do not know."

Oh, how he jumps up!

"What kind of comrade am I to you?"

I don't know what to say. I really don't. How can I, a village girl, know? When I was born we all lived under Polish rule. The only Russian words I have heard are "comrade, comrade."

Up until I ended up in camp, I did not know that you had to say: "Citizen." Immediately after the war, while I was still living in a village, I was just a simple country girl. When I ended up in camp, I found out that I was a 'counter-revolutionary'. We only heard this in the camps.

My investigation did not last long. I was taken on March 2nd. The trial was around April 17th. After the trial we were immediately assigned to execution cells. I was sentenced to 15 years of hard labour. Once you were sentenced to hard labour, you were put in special cells. It was only possible to get into the cell by crawling on your side, because the chain on the door was so thick. And the floor was cement. You cannot imagine the fear.

Then through the air hole someone call to us: "Who are you?"

We answer: "We are women, girls."

And they tell us: "We are boys. We have been sentenced to death. We are on death row."

* * * * *

In the middle of May we were taken out and brought to Kharkiv. There a group of us were gathered for transport. We were loaded into freight carriages and brought straight to Nakhodka. Summer had begun already. It was hot in those carriages. The train moved for a while, then it stopped. It stood still. Later it moved on again. We were fed, but it was irregular. Once, it was obvious that we had been given something that was not very fresh. There was an outbreak of dysentery. And so we travelled with the sickness, we travelled like that for a whole month, right up through to June, when we arrived in Nakhodka. Just then we heard on the radio that Kalinin had died. This was when we arrived in Nakhodka.

We were settled in barracks. We were allowed to go outside. After prison, and after these freight carriages, as soon as we went out in the sun, we all burned. It was awful. And then malaria struck. How we began to fear malaria! We lay side by side. Again I did not think that I would live, but I survived.

Later, when the second month started, we were put into brigades and made to work. We were taken to dig up potatoes. Sometimes we were allowed to bake a few potatoes in the fire. Somehow we baked the potatoes. Then we were also given fish. We ate so well, I began to think: "Perhaps they will leave us here."

Autumn came. It was October and they said: "Gather your things. You are leaving." And we were loaded onto some ship. I do not know its name. I don't know because it never entered my mind to look at the inscription on the ship. Yes, it was autumn, already evening, and there were such black clouds. When we were loaded into the hold, it was already dark. How we sailed! How we were tossed about! The ship pitched so! We lay side by side – we could only lie there. I think we were given something to eat, but I do not remember. We wanted to drink. Maybe we were given water, maybe we weren't. I don't remember anything. I only remember when it became clear that we were arriving in Magadan. It had just begun to freeze slightly. There was hoar frost on the handrails and on the deck. We tried to scratch it off with our hands in order to at least moisten our mouths.

We arrived and were unloaded at Nagayevo. It was cold and there was a layer of frost. We were marched right away to Transportnaia Street. There was a bathhouse there. As we were led along the road, we all grabbed snow to put in our mouths since we were so parched. How sick we were, sapped of any energy! They washed us, dressed us in pea-coats. Our number was sewn on the back, from sleeve to sleeve. My number was L-221. They did not give us trousers, neither winter nor summer trousers. Nor did they give us boots. Nothing. We remained in our own clothes, whatever we had.

When we were still in Nakhodka and our brigade was taken out to dig potatoes, I would bring a few back and treat our group. A different brigade went to sort out the storehouse. And one woman gave me a sweater, probably a man's sweater, already all torn – only the arms were whole. I wore those sleeves on my legs. I tied them up with string. Only this sweater saved my legs. Other girls remained in tights, or in whatever they had when they were brought here.

Ninety of us girls were brought into the *taiga*, to the uranium mine at Butugichag. We were brought to Ust-Omchug, then still a little farther to Butugichag by truck. There it was all mountains, mountains all around, and only a rail along which small carts ran. And in the summer there were possibly some steps. But in the winter we slid down the mountain right on our bottoms. We were brought to Butugichag, and then still farther and farther and then down. There was a factory, Karmen, there, but we were taken still farther, past Karmen.

We were put in barracks. It was tremendously cold. In the middle of the barracks was a barrel, but there was no fuel to make a fire, because there was no firewood there, nothing. This was in the camp, Vakhanka. There we were given a few clothes. We were given padded cotton pants and shoes, boots, not even felt boots, we called them *burki*. They were sewn from the same fabric as the pea-coats.

We were assigned to work in the forest. We were given toboggans. There was a wire fastened to the toboggan and a stick wrapped in the wire, a long stick so that two people could be harnessed. We were ordered to bring back two cubic metres of firewood on each trip. A woman was waiting when we arrived back and measured how much wood we had brought. The bundle needed to be one metre high and two metres long. That was two cubic metres for one trip. Then there was soup for us. We ate and we went back again with the empty toboggan. And again we would bring back two cubic metres. Four cubic metres per day was the norm.

In the morning we were given perhaps 17 ounces of bread, tea and sometimes a little piece of herring. I ate half of the bread right away, and the other half I carried with me, here by my bosom, for lunch. In the evening we were given another seven ounces of bread. Sometimes in the morning we were given *kasha*. In the beginning there was not even a spoon. It was evident that before us, men had lived there. When they left, they had taken everything. We made these little bowls from tin cans and scooped up our kasha with bread. Two or three mouthfuls and it was gone.

And we are still hungry. But there is still a half piece of bread. And I carry this firewood and I feel that there is this little piece of black bread tucked in there, so I eat it all up, see.

And I drag this toboggan.

It is heavy.

I strain with all my might. I push with my chest.

We must choose a partner who is the same height, because if one is tall and one is short, how is it for her? The harness falls at the stomach for one and at the throat for the other. The stick has to be harnessed evenly. Otherwise, the tall woman pushes with her chest on the stick, moves it away from herself, and all the weight falls on the short woman.

This is how we work.

And then we bring the toboggan to the camp on foot. We go out to assemble and line up in columns with the guard – heads down, arms behind our backs. A step to the right, a step to the left, they will shoot. I do not feel morally like a person. In general, we forgot that we are people.

Well, later, when we go into the camp, at least there is the stick of firewood that I freely carried back so that there is kindling and towards morning I will have dried at least something, at least my mittens. And so I can warm the cup of water given to me and at least wash a bit.

After a year, all of us who had arrived together were all shrivelled up. Our supervisor, when we first came, had tried to persuade us: "Girls, do not drink much water. You will be hungry and want to eat." There was a boiler there, and yes, there was always boiled water. Whoever could not endure the hunger poured this water into her soup. Then her legs swelled up. They told us right away: "Girls, just don't drink much. And if you hold out a year, you will adapt. You will become acclimatised."

* * * * *

Well, we dragged the toboggans like this for a year or two. In the summer we were all prepared to continue cutting the firewood. Instead we were sent to the pit-face. We would rake up the ore at the pit-face. After the explosives went off, it was ventilated a little bit, and then we went in with shovels, into the coffin that is what it was known as.

We rake and load the ore into little wagons.

It's dark here.

There are no respirators, no helmets. It is frightening where the stone hangs.

It's dark like an oven.

On the sides are barrels with rags soaked in some kind of fuel, which they light. These torches burn. There is a stench and a stuffiness. We have to breathe this, and continue raking.

Strength – I have no strength.

My strength pours out.

* * * * *

In the winter, it was back to the toboggans again. Then in 1947 while I dragged a toboggan, I developed scurvy. All of my teeth fell out. I began to suffer night blindness. I could not see anything. I still had to go to work. During the day I would drag a toboggan. I could still see a little, but as it got dark, while I was returning from work, I couldn't see anything. It was unbelievable. I was young – 22, 23, 24 years old, but I couldn't see. Whoever could still see would lead the others. She would say: "Here's your bunk. Lie down."

Somehow I got sent to the medical unit. I was panting very heavily. This small woman, Mariika, cleaned there. She said: "Help me carry the water." This was our brigade's day off. I helped her carry water from the river. I helped her clean everything. And she poured some fish oil for me, maybe a half of a glass. She poured it into a test tube. I hid it on the bunk under a little shirt that I still had from home. I would keep a little piece of bread from dinner and dip it in. I ate the fish oil that way for a week, maybe, and I began to see again.

How thin we were! We were taken to the bathhouse every nine days. We would come back from work and – "Quickly, quickly, girls, to the bathhouse!" In the bathhouse, we would undress – just blue tendons were visible; ribs and skin. We were not like women. And even such womanly matters did not occur. Lord, how we looked! It was not possible to tie up our pants even with string. It never held. And I panted very heavily. Already my bronchial tubes, it seems, were so beaten up, so ill.

My cheeks were so frostbitten that blisters appeared. Liquid oozed from them. I wore a hat on your head, but under your hat I breathed. The cold was severe and my cheeks were completely frostbitten.

We were given foot bindings. I tore off a piece of the foot binding, washed it, and tied it liked a scarf under my hat. I would come back from work, dry it by the stove and tie it under my hat again.

That is how we worked – in the winters on toboggans, in the summer, if not at the pit-face, then we gathered sand. We did this when one of the little carts turned over or spilled somewhere. We gathered it up. There were rails – two rows of rails here and there. The loaded carts would go down and the empty ones come up. Those little wagons could fly. Those of us who worked there at the plant had to pull them. These carts loaded with ore were such big boxes. We gathered the sand where the carts turned over and carried it to the plant. We worked on a team of three people. One jigged it. She poured it into a box and jigged it with a trough; the other two carried the sand. Later we would switch, because the water was cold. Our hands were in the cold water. It was necessary to produce 4.41 pounds of this metal.

I remember once, at the pit-face, a girl saw a little stone above, probably barren rock, but it seemed that there was some metal there that had turned black. She climbed up to look. She stepped on a stone, on one, then on another – and then it caved in! We were immediately taken out of the pit. They said that all her bones were broken.

There were also cobblestones everywhere and nothing to brace this stone. There was no earth, just rocky layers. When we carried the ore to the plant, if we needed to set up a light in order to see, you had to dig out this stone, pull everything out from inside, put the pole in, and then pack it with snow and stone to reinforce it. It was hellish work!

Someone once asked me if we had lice. We had no lice there. Such parasites love warmth and to eat well. But what did we have on us to eat? Bones! And the cold was such that you could not warm up!

Eventually I was brought from logging to the plant at Karmen for good. There the men from the pit-face, from the gallery, brought their loads up to the mountain. At the plant we took it, sorted it, and threw out the barren rock. There was a unit for crushing this waste stone. And the dust! We were stationed nearby and had no choice but to breathe this dust. There was no protective equipment – what kind of protective equipment could there be?

The conveyor belt would run the whole day. There the ore was loaded. Then the crushing machine crushed this stone. We would load 12 wagons, and then the engine would take this wagon and bring it to the plant called Chapaev. This was the jigging plant.

Girls worked at the plant as welders and metal workers. They did it all and in temperatures of minus 58 degrees Fahrenheit. They worked in two shifts – a night shift and a day shift. After logging, this work was a little easier for me, at least a little bit. It was possible to step outside of the plant. There was a barrel there which had a fire burning in it. So it was possible to at least warm your hands a little. The plant was cold, but at least it was not the forest.

* * * * *

And so it was while Stalin was alive. In 1953 Stalin died. Our numbers were removed. For many years we hadn't heard our own name or surname – only L-221, L-222, L-223. We would go out for roll call. We would drag the toboggans in pairs, and yet we rarely knew each other's name. We hauled them in silence – our names forgotten.

But when Stalin died, our numbers were removed. And bread was put on the table for us. We would come in and there would be bread on the table. We grabbed the bread to our bosom, hiding from one another, thinking only of ourselves first. We thought that it was being given just this once. But later there was bread on the table again. How hungry we had been before this! We would stand in line for bread and it would seem that someone was given a little more bread. "Oh, she received more than I did. She has a little stick stuck to her bread to make weight, but I don't." We didn't think about anything else, had no other thoughts – not that I am still young, not that I might still return to Mama – only about a little piece of black bread! It is impossible to compare with anything. It is similar to a hungry beast. He sees food, his eyes are blazing. And like him, we only thought about bread and how to get it. That was it.

After work we would come back from logging and, in turn, we would bring water to the kitchen for the cauldrons, for soup, for tea. After such work! And I would still get upset that I didn't manage to be picked this time. They only took six girls. Two drag the toboggans, two push from behind. Those who were chosen would pour the water from the river into barrels and then pour it again into cauldrons. And so on, all night.

Towards morning, we were given a small bowl of *kasha* – just a little bowl of *kasha*! – and it would already be cold. We would go home in the morning and the morning call would already be playing. It would be time for work. I would think: "God, I still need to dry my mittens. They're wet from the water." We were ready to work around the clock, if only to eat a bit. It is impossible to describe how difficult it was. The conditions were completely inhumane. There is nothing with which even to compare it.

And this was not just a year or two of hunger. I had been so hungry since the war started. It was the whole of my youth – the whole time.

* * * * *

1954 started. We were still working there at Vakhanka. Later in 1954 we were brought to Kinkhandzha. There was an ore concentration plant there too. We worked there. Then we were brought to Magadan to work on building projects.

It was warmer there. The cold was not so bad. All around Magadan stood these high fences and sometime someone going by would throw a loaf of bread over the fence. So then we were more sated, having eaten at least a little bread.

And it is easier than in the forest, even though it is building work and it is January; and we are digging foundation trenches by hand.

One holds this iron wedge and another beats it with a sledge hammer.

What have you managed to dig out? You beat, beat, beat, and you have only reached the thawed earth, but it is time to go home.

It is so frustrating.

And we worked on the mortar mixer. It was difficult, but nevertheless, it wasn't like it was in the forest.

We built Magadan Pre-School number 52, School number four, and the technical institute. I even saved a photograph. I remember that we had a brigade leader, a German – Ziber, I think was his surname – Andrei Yakovich. We asked him to have his photograph taken with us. And he said: "Really, girls! I have a very jealous wife." I remember various incidents, trifles. How many people were with me at Vakhanka and here on construction – Latvians, Lithuanians, Estonians! What conscientious, hardworking, honest people they were! How much I respected them! They were very good people. They treated one another so well.

And so we built during 1955. 1956 started and we built Nursery number 11. Then we also had a good foreman, Aleksandr Aleksandrovich. We were told that a commission from Moscow was arriving. And suddenly on May 6th, we were not led out to work, to the brigade. We were brought to the military base. This is where the soldiers and military had been stationed. They called us one at a time. They asked us everything, even if our mothers were at home. And then they said that we could go home. They gave us money right away – 100 roubles for the ship and 70 roubles for the train.

But where can we go?

How can I go home from a building site and in an old torn jersey and hat?

And I'm now 32 years old. Thirty two years old! My youth has passed.

I remember there had been a man named Krilov as the head of the camp. He was such a malicious one. He said: "You will still fall. And when you fall, they won't pick you up." Later, Levchenko was head of the camp. He was a little softer and he began to advise us.

"Girls, when you carry this building material, have two people stand up under the ends. You are future mothers, remember this!"

The idea arose in my mind for a moment that indeed we were women. My God, I no longer knew who I was. We were herded to and from work. And you went and you thought: "Should I eat the bread that I left for lunch now? No, what would there be for lunch?" There was no soup, just water. If there were oats, then the water was all muddied from the grain, and if it was pea soup, then there was just a pea chasing a pea. My God, how you always wanted to eat! It is inconceivable – to have lived like that for years! A young organism! Excessive work!

Then they released us all. We returned to the barrack. There were 12 of us. There was no convoy guard! How confused we were, like chicks without the hen. We were completely perplexed. It was frightening to go out. How many years had we gone out only with a guard?

The first days we were lost. We were completely unaccustomed to the fact that you could simply go out, that you needed to decide something by yourself. Yes, and it was – it has to be said – an evil time. They released the political prisoners, but also many common criminals and rogues.

These thugs even called on us first. It was late; they knocked. The girls asked: "Who is it?" They answered it was the military and we opened the door. Two bandits were standing there, but when they saw how many of us there were, they left. So for the first months, the guards continued to look after this barrack. We requested this ourselves.

Later I met a woman who, in the camps, had given out work assignments, a bit like a cadre officer. She suggested: "Go and work at the milk plant." I agreed with joy. Of course! And she sent me immediately for a medical examination and assigned me work there and then. We continued to live in the same barrack, only the room was a little smaller. This housing was legally given to us as workers. One girl worked at the chicken farm, another in the greenhouses, and I at the milk plant. We brought ourselves back something to eat and it now became easier for us. We now earned money. I even celebrated by buying a light overcoat for myself. I bought a dress. We already began to somehow come alive!

* * * * *

After a few weeks we went with one girl whom we worked with to get a passport with her certificate of release.

And a young man approaches me. He comes with his friend.

He approaches me and says: "Help me get a job. I went to find a room. I wanted to live at one place, but the landlord says that he will not register bachelors.

"Help me. We'll say that we are now husband and wife, that we just married, so that he will give me a registration document."

Well, I agree.

We go to the landlord and tell him. And he, it's true, registers Yuri. And he is able to get a job at the bread factory.

That's how we met. And soon we registered our marriage, sometime within the month. Why not? He was 32 and I was 32. We were married, but where could we live? He would come to me in the dormitory, but there all men had to leave at 11pm. My husband was advised to rent a room from one landlady on Transportnaia Street. She had her own house. She accepted renters for 300 roubles a month. We went to live there.

We bought a bucket, two small mugs, two spoons, and now, happy, we began our life together. Neither he nor I had any money, but we were happy. There was something to eat with and something to begin with. It was still necessary to cut your own firewood, to stoke the oven, and to fetch your own water. Once, when I was pregnant, I was carrying water. It was almost time to give birth. And I fell very hard. Our landlady said: "What are we going to do with you? I don't know."

But everything turned out well. The doctors were surprised at me, having been starved for so long, giving birth. How had a child survived in these famished bones? Yet, my daughter was born. I was lying in the hospital and thinking: "At least they did not discharge me yet. How will it be nursing an infant in a cold room?" I was afraid, really afraid. Could I really be a mother? Could I really do it? I had no milk in my breasts. I bottle-fed the baby. I had to buy milk all the time from people who had a cow. I was lying in the hospital afraid that I did not know how to do anything with a child. But, true, our landlady was good. She treated us well. She said, "No one has paid me money as reliably as you." My husband, as soon as he received his pay, immediately paid her. Whatever was left remained for us.

So she gave milk to my husband for me in the birthing house. She had a cow. And when we were discharged, she showed me how to bathe my daughter, how to put her nappies on. So we lived with her for some time. Then one of my husband's comrades who worked with him offered us his room, since he was leaving. It was in the former women's barrack. And we moved there immediately, even before he left. As before it was still necessary to stoke the stove, cut firewood and carry water. We lived there for seven years.

* * * * *

In 1959, my husband, daughter and I went to Mama in Ukraine. By that time, my Mama had already buried me twice. The first time someone had written to the village where grandmother lived saying that a woman from the village had died in Vakhanka and that she only had a mother. Mama thought that this was me. At that time she held a wake for me. And then the second time, when she had no letters from me for a long time – I was already in Magadan; I was already married! – again she thought that I was no longer alive. Twice she thought that I had died. Oh, Gracious God, what my mother endured! She wrote to me here, when I was already in Magadan: "I do not want anything but to hear one word from you; to hear you say 'Mama'."

Oh, how she met us when we came that first time! We arrived on the feast of Peter and Paul. She fell on her knees. She was crying and only said: "Lord, you have given me such joy on the feast of Peter and Paul." She took our daughter, her granddaughter by the hand. Well, the whole village cried. So much had come to pass!

We wanted to stay in Ukraine and live. But after living there a little while, we understood that it was not any better there. It was impossible to find work – there was a special note in our passports. Mama's house had a straw roof. The war and all the years had completely destroyed it. Who would have repaired it for Mama all those years? The rain came. It flowed in through the roof. We carried our child in our arms. But mainly there was no work anywhere. Everywhere there were collective farms, state farms, but the people were barely surviving. My husband said: "We're going back!"

Yes, we returned. I began to take care of yet another child. I was sitting with my own. I took another. Back then it was difficult to get into a nursery. They paid me 50 roubles a month. I had to get up early to start the fire in the stove so that it was already warm when they brought the child. I nursed my own and nursed another.

My husband also worked during the day and if possible he worked at night. When the reforms came in 1961, he went to the storehouses to select books and rewrite them at night. He went to work everywhere that he could to earn some money. We saved a little money and again went to my Mama's. Even here my husband did not rest. He went and ordered a vehicle and brought stone. We began to build a little house for my mother. It was a pity to look at my elderly mother. And to bring her back here to the north – she was over 80! Where could she live? The conditions in which we ourselves lived were no good.

Once we had begun to build a little house for Mama, we needed to somehow accumulate money to send to her, at least a little. Mama also kept chickens. She sold eggs. She too saved money. Later Mama was so old that she could not carry water from the well for herself. She needed firewood for the winter; and someone needed to cut it for her. In that way many years passed while we built Mama her little house.

It is interesting – once a gypsy told Mama her future and said: "You work. You work. But there will be no one to look after you and to pity you." And then: "Oh, you will also live in a new house." Forty years passed and after 40 years, Mama entered her new home.

We built such a good home for Mama. True, it was heated with a wood stove. The village, after all, may still have wood stoves for heating even now. Mama said: "I am so grateful. I am on my knees, on my knees. I went into my new house and sat on the stove, and how good it was." Later we sent Mama money in order to help her with the firewood for the oven and carrying water from the well.

And so it was all the time. We needed money to send to Mama and to send our daughter to school. I received 70 roubles as a hospital orderly. My husband received 9, working as a storeman.

Finally we received an apartment here. It was 1964. Our daughter was already big and went to school. She no longer sat on a little chamber pot, but went to the outhouse. How much suffering, my God! We went to my husband's factory to bathe – that is, if there was a good guard on duty, we were able to bathe. My husband said: "Let's have more children." What? Lord, the poor Russian women! How much on this earth must a person endure!

So in 1964, we got given our apartment. There was a supervisor in the mayor's office, Karpov was his surname. He came to meet us. After seven years, after the barracks, we received keys to our own apartment. We went to pick up our daughter at school. We brought her back. She poured water into the bathtub and said: "Perhaps this is a dream. Perhaps this is not true."

That is how we lived.

We saved and saved money, just a little – what money did we have to save from? When our daughter was 20 years old, in 1977, we say: "Here are 5,000 roubles. We put it for you in this book. Let it be for a rainy day." And what happened? They are there in this book even now. *Perestroika* began. There were various monetary re-valuations. Everything was lost. And that's what is funny. That's how it was my whole life. Even before the war, under Poland, Mama was working, working. She sold eggs. She sold a piglet. She put aside a little money, so that there would be at least something for clothing. And she was no longer young.

Then the Russians came, and *złoty*, Polish money, were no longer needed; roubles were. We had just accumulated these roubles, when the Germans came and then we needed marks. Mama exchanged eggs for a few marks. But then the Russian returned to power again, and we went back to roubles. You see how much was all lost.

What happened then happened now. And so it was my whole life! So much human labour wasted! You look and already we are elderly. And that is all. We try to live on our pensions –this, after all, is old age.

And I remember my whole life like this, with no depth to it. Gracious God, after all, every year, beginning with childhood, I worked for the rich. You bend. Your back hurts unbearably. You cannot wait until they say: "Sit and eat." You come home, and so many more things have to be done at home. Quickly, quickly while Mama fires up the stove, I milk the cow or vice versa. Later the milk boils and we quickly mix two eggs with flour. You pour it into the milk and cook it like noodle soup. I will always remember this. Oh, how delicious it was! Such was our life.

You recall, but to recall is frightening. I only knew how to tend the cow, to work on the farm, to look after my home and my Mama. There was no time for studying. I was the girl of a poor widow. I did not have a father or an older brother. We were trying to survive all the time. I understood this very early on. What is there to say?

I lived just 15 years of my life before the war – 15! And then my childhood ended and war began. And after the war, the prison camps. The camps ended, we only knew work. I was so exhausted. Yet, if it was possible, you took another part-time position. When my daughter studied at the institute, she substituted for those who went on vacation and worked herself. Sometimes you come home with high blood pressure, your heart hurts, your bronchial tubes are not working right…

Now in Church there are meetings for those of us who were repressed. We need this so much! At least now we have been noticed! I am truly enriched. I go and I tell my daughter and my granddaughter everything – how good, how simple the meetings are, both the concerts and tea. I tell them all the news from the people.

In the past we were afraid to approach a priest. But Fr Michael, you know, is such a gift from God. I cannot even explain to my daughter or granddaughter how holy and humble this person is. For the elderly he is like a thoughtful son. And these meetings are so needed. I worked so much – what kind of community was there in the face of such hard work? How many of these people did I turn over, like rags and sacks, as a hospital orderly? But here I have become acquainted with so many people who suffered like me. I even found my fellow-countrymen, even those from my region.

After release, even though we lived in Magadan, we did not know or see each other. You understand – work, marriage, children, worries and then grandchildren. Here we have become acquainted. Here is a quiet, somehow bright community. We need these meetings now very much.

That is how my whole life was lived. Such a life – an eternal struggle for survival. I always said that I worked as long as I remember from need, and I ate only when possible. Understand – that was the one constant of my whole life.

Yuri Aleksandrovich Portnov

Born:	October 24th 1924
Where:	Vladivostok
Country:	USSR
Arrested:	1948
Sentence:	25 year corrective labour, plus 5 years loss of political and civil rights
Released:	August 18th 1956

I WAS BORN ON OCTOBER 24th 1924 IN THE CITY OF VLADIVOSTOK. I was an only child.

When I was four years old, that is in 1928, people were recruited to go to work on the Chinese Eastern Railway. So I, along with my parents, moved to Xarbin, a large industrial city, where at that time lived over 300,000 Russians. Overall it was a city of a million people in the middle of China, or as it was then called, Manchuria.

At the beginning of the 1930's they started to send the Russians back. But quite a lot of people preferred to remain there in Xarbin, as they heard that people were starving in the Soviet Union at that time. And so in order to remain, they got immigration passports and settled there for good.

In Xarbin at that time, there were more than 10 churches. In the very centre of the city, there was a beautiful cathedral, built all of wood, without a single nail being used in its construction. They took our entire class there for Easter service.

We were all believers.

Not only was the Orthodox Church present in Xarbin, but also the Catholic Church. There was a Catholic school there, known as the Christian academy. They only accepted Catholics in this academy, and you had to pay a lot of money. We always had friendly relations with them, competing in different types of sports.

I went to an all boy Russian school. It was a large school, with 10 grades. I completed my studies there at 16 and enrolled in the Northern-Manchurian University.

Unlike school, one had to pay a certain amount of money to go to the university. I studied there two years. All the students wore a red uniform, and only those wearing that uniform were allowed on campus.

My parents began to have financial troubles, and so like all students, I decided to earn a little extra money during vacation. And so I worked ferrying people across the river. We received 10 *kopeks* per person. There was a convenient place where one could rent a boat for a rouble for the whole day. So I thought I would do that, as one didn't need any special training.

But after a couple of days I discovered that there were lots of ferrymen, but few passengers. I had to work all day long till my hands ached and only earned enough for lunch. So that was enough of that!

As autumn approached, and the new school year was looming, a friend told me that they were hiring guards at the railway station. They pay was 200 roubles, imagine! Bread cost us just 22 *kopeks*. Two hundred roubles was very good pay. And so I went there, not telling my parents anything. I thought I would earn some money, and then tell them, and then when I returned again, I would finish my education. It was 1943.

Three of us were hired, an older family man, myself and Tolik (he was another young man, like me). They divided us up, assigning whom to watch when, but later we started to change our shifts ourselves, working out who was on duty at night and who during the day.

I worked until August 1945; I had sent a letter to my parents, but never received a reply.

Then on one of those August days, three Japanese soldiers came. One spoke perfect Russian. He announced that there was war. The Red Army was approaching, and therefore no one should go anywhere. There was a building there, similar to a dormitory with single rooms, standing like garages next to one another. And around them stood a two-metre-high brick wall.

They locked the gate, and said: it's dangerous, don't go out. We'll close it just in case. The night passed and in the morning I went out and looked: Japanese sentries surrounded the fence.

I could hear a deep rumbling sound in the distance. Our tanks were coming!

* * * * *

I climb the wall and head toward the rumble.

I see dust rising in the road; the tanks were coming nearer.

I stand and gaze, mouth open. Interesting.

The head tank stops. A soldier comes out and asks: "Do you understand Russian?"

"I speak Russian."

"Oh, you're Russian! Do you know the way to Port Artur?"

I answer: "Of course I know, how could I not? You simply have to follow the signs. They're everywhere showing where you need to go. In English."

The tank driver asks: "And do you know English?"

"I know conversational English, Japanese, and Chinese."

He says; "Climb in, come with us."

Then I ask: "Can I get my stuff?"

"Where? What stuff?"

"At the factory," I say.

"There's a factory here?"

"Yes," I say, "over there, with Japanese soldiers".

He turns the tank and heads there. We come up to the factory. There's a large metal gate, with Japanese sentries. The tank comes straight up, pointing its gun at them, and the commander orders: "Surrender, Japan must capitulate."

The Japanese don't understand anything. I translate into Japanese the best I can. They understand me and ask to be given an hour while they consider.

Almost an hour passes, and the tank commander points the gun and says: "Will you open the gates now? If you don't put down your weapons, we'll shoot.

So I translate, and after several minutes the gate opens and a soldier and officer come out.

They come out and throw down their weapons. Well, our soldiers are armed with automatic machine guns, and the Japanese only have poorer weapons.

The search goes well. Soon a captain arrives in a car. They report that such and such was done, and that these lads had helped.

The captain asks: "Are you planning on staying or coming with us?"

I answer, "What sense is there in staying here? The factory is obviously closed."

"Okay," he says, "come with me."

I sit in the car and we go. He brings me to the army headquarters. They need a translator.

I tell them: "I'm not a very good translator."

No one argues with me. I silently accept their decision: I will be a translator.

* * * * *

I moved along with the headquarters, farther and farther along battle lines. Then they ordered me to work in the commandant's office, translating for supply.

I would go to the markets to haggle with the Chinese.

I worked like this for several months. Then they suggested that I move to the city of Dalni, or in Chinese, Dalyan. There I was enlisted as a soldier in

106

the 39th cannon division. I served there until 1948. It was a quiet time; everyone awaited demobilisation.

Somehow the conversation got around to where everyone would be going. Someone planned on going to a communal farm. I said I would never go to a farm.

"Why not?"

"Because I'm a city boy. I don't know anything about farms, and would be no use there - so why go there?"

It happened that I had argued with an older lieutenant by the name of Smirnov. He called me a 'yobbo'. And I said that he was a 'yobbo' himself.

Then he threatened me: "You'll always remember me."

And so, either because of the talk about the farm, or because I argued with him, unfortunate events were about to happen to me.

* * * * *

About a week later, they called me to come immediately to headquarters. Well, I worked there, of course I thought they needed something translated.

I went there without concern. But as soon as I arrived I was thrown immediately into a cell, and then taken for questioning. I was held for over a month. They didn't ask me about anything. They had no material of any sort.

"You haven't told us everything."

"Think about it."

"We need more, be more precise."

I was calm, trusting in my innocence. I was never in any kind of political party. I never cooperated with the Germans, because I never saw them, except at the movies. All the time they treated me badly. The interrogator at last announced: "We've finished our investigation, read this and sign it."

I read it.

In the place marked 'school attended' is written: "Counter-revolutionary school."

I ask: "Why counter-revolutionary"?

"Well," the interrogator answers, "after all, it wasn't a soviet school."

"That doesn't make it counterrevolutionary", I say.

He isn't interested. It was counter-revolutionary because it wasn't soviet.

His entire case against me is like that.

When I was sat in my cell, I had tried to imagine the reason for my arrest. I thought perhaps it was because I had written an essay in a school exam which had won first place, and was read out before the entire school. In it I had written that this was my second homeland. I told the investigator about it.

"You see!" he rejoices. "Counter-revolutionary agitation."

I ask him: "Why was it counter-revolutionary? After all I wrote that it was my second, and that my first was the Soviet Union."

"But you wrote that things are good here," he replies. "You studied here".

"What's so bad," I object to him, "that I studied here and went about my life peacefully. I have friends here."

"Here's a second article for you," the investigator concludes. The first charge, I think, changing countries, is against Article 58.

* * * * *

Once at the prison in Port Artur, they led us all outside.

We lined up and one of the officers explained that on account of the prisoners' complaints, a representative of the tribunal had come, and anyone who had any questions should please ask them.

Everyone had their questions about how they were feeding us and when would they be sending us on elsewhere.

I raise my hand.

The major, the representative of the war tribunal, comes up to me and so I ask him: "My investigation has finished; when will my trial be? Why hasn't there been a trial yet?"

He asks my name.

I tell him.

"Oh, Portnov," he notes. "The war tribunal has already looked at your case, and for lack of evidence you should soon be released. So don't worry. I'll send your case to Khabarovsk, to the regional authorities, just wait a bit. The war tribunal has rejected your case for lack of evidence."

I am so relieved.

Several days pass, and again the lead us all outside and line us up.

They are to announce the decisions of the judges.

They begin with the lesser crimes – thievery and drunkenness.

Then for accusations under Article 58: Petrov – 25 years; Portnov – 25 years.

It was signed by the tribunal of the NKGB of the Khabarovsk region.

And so I would return to my homeland – only now as a prisoner. On the second night my cellmate looked at me and said: "Yurka, your hair is white." I had greyed in one night.

* * * * *

After several days, they took all the prisoners at the Port Artur prison who had received sentences of 25 years to Vladivostok in the brigs of war ships. This was 1948, the same year I was arrested.

I was taken to my home city, and put in prison. When they brought us from the port, we were transported in vehicles without windows, so I didn't even get a sight of my home town. It was the same in our cells – bars and a little peep hole. It was made small on purpose so that we could see nothing out of the window. You couldn't even reach it, the little window was located so high up, just under the ceiling.

From my hometown I was soon sent by stages to Irkutsk, to work on the Taishet-Bratsk railway. We were taken deep into the *taiga*. There was a camp there, and we were made to cut lumber. The conditions were horrible. We got thinner and thinner from near starvation.

The work was back-breaking. One cut the trees, another trimmed the branches, and another hauled these logs to the railroad. You take a log, try to lift it, and you can't. You need 10 to 12 men to lift one log.

Trying to lift a log, you tremble and think: "Please God, don't let me fall under such weight, don't let it crush me." And yet we survived even that.

When I was sent to this camp, there were criminals, murderers and thieves there. Terror reigned. To look on them, with their scarred features, bestial behaviour, and foul language, was very difficult for me. I had never broken the law in my life, nor seen the criminal world up close, but now found myself suddenly thrown in the thick of such people.

I think that affected my psyche more than the hard work.

And it was more than a little cold. Oh, such cold! I survived even that. Many criminals, in order to avoid the hard work, would cut off their own finger. If they cut off either a toe or a finger, or in some other way maimed themselves, they would be like an invalid, and sit in camp. They might bind books or be given some other light duty.

I was late for roll call once. The brigade had been called to the zone and counted when I ran up. That was it, they wouldn't let me go. I was immediately put in manacles, and beaten, leaving welts on my shoulders. I was sent to the harsh regime barrack.

Usually this barrack held only murderers and prisoners who had committed horrible crimes. They were not sent on work assignments, no one even touched them, everyone was so afraid of them, even the camp officials themselves. Even the guards refused to take them to work. And so, because they wouldn't allow me to work, I spent some time in this hard regime barrack, sitting with murderers.

They played cards there. There was no money there, so these bandits bet on people. The games lasted for hours. The loser was supposed to kill someone.

I sat in the barrack and thought: "Are they betting on me, or have they chosen someone else to kill?"

I spent two weeks there and, thankfully no one laid a hand on me.

* * * * *

One day they called everyone out into the zone, telling us to bring all our possessions. They called roll, and checked everyone out. Then we were put into vehicles and sent again to Taishet; from there we were put in railway carriages and taken to the port of Vanino.

On arrival we saw camps one after the other. Where one zone ended another began.

Only I didn't see a lot of anything there. It all blurred into one terrible dream for me. Other Russian prisoners, who had always lived here, knew more than we who came from other countries.

I had the impression that I was among the insane or terrible criminals, who, as they say, are beyond words.

But little by little I got used to it.

* * * * *

We were at the port of Vanino at the beginning of summer of 1950.

In June, they called the prisoners sentenced under Article 58. We were sent on board the steamer *Dzhurma*. Then they filled up the rest of the hold with common criminals, and shipped us to Magadan.

We sailed for five or six days. We disembarked on the hills of Marchican. We were gathered up, surrounded by guards with dogs and sent to the zone.

Then roll call: they call all those condemned under Article 58. We can only confirm our status – Article 58, paragraphs 4 and 10, 25-year sentence. Everyone whom they listed in Port Artur had 25-year sentences and five years deprived of rights.

We were packed on cattle trucks and sent up the highway. There were probably at least 10 of those vehicles. It was a long way. Once in a while along the way, one of the prisoners would recognise somewhere and there would be talk that we were being sent to some sort of large construction project, something very important, where they would feed us well.

They brought us to the village of Myaundzh in the Susaman region, and there, as we already knew, we would be building an electric power plant. But at that time they had only just built the camp; everything else was completely empty. The main construction was just getting started.

The next day, they gave us new padded jackets, new pea-jackets, boots, large mattresses, and even pillow cases. My new camp uniform carried the number B2-572, sewn on the cap, the pants and back of the padded jacket.

Then they took us to a field and told us to cut the grass, and dry it like hay, so that we could stuff our mattresses and pillows.

* * * * *

Construction began. We dug a large foundation ditch. We dug it in the autumn, but then winter began, and so we also dug in the winter – by hand and with picks. The ground was 'category four' – the most difficult kind of land. There were large, paving size stones there and the earth was frozen solid.

Finally they realised that we could thaw the ground with fire. We were allowed to light bonfires at night. We covered them with pieces of metal so that the ground would thaw faster. Digging became easier.

I worked as a 'driver', pushing my 'vehicle' – called an 'Asso'. It was a simple wheelbarrow – two handles, one wheel. They filled my wheelbarrow with dirt, I pushed it 50 metres to empty it, went back, and they filled it again. And that was my routine, all day long – 10 hours a day.

We returned to the zone very tired, of course. Of course, they didn't give us just 20 ounces of bread, as they did in Irkutsk working on the Taishet-Bratsk rail line; now we received a whole 28 ounces! We would receive an extra portion of mush if we did more than 100 percent of our quota, and even triple portions for 125 percent fulfilment of quota. We never once received triple portions – where could one find the strength to do such a workload? – but doubles, yes, sometimes we earned double portions.

* * * * *

It was already 1955.

I was encouraged a bit at this camp. There were only people sentenced under Article 58 here, all normal people. There were no thieves or murderers among us, none of their ugly disfigurements, no foul language. Everyone worked, everyone was peaceful. There were many Latvians and Lithuanians and everyone worked.

After five years the groundwork was completed. They only left carpenters, cement workers, and plasterers. All the rest – including me – who didn't have any building experience were sent by truck to the end of the road, to Indigurk.

There was a mine there in which they dug out ore extract, which affected one's lungs. After a year and a half, people became invalids. They were listed as invalids and sent on light duty.

They put me on the sorting line, where all the mined ore would go by and I would have to sort it. If we find ore with sparkles, we put it on the side; all the rest went on the slag heap.

People usually only worked on this sorting for six or seven months and no more. Your lungs simply hardened, such that you couldn't breathe in or out, you became completely incapacitated. I worked there for half a year.

* * * * *

113

In 1956 they sent us away. The chose us, the young, convicts and those with short sentences (some sentenced under Article 58 were given only 10 years) and brought us all to Magadan.

We didn't know where we were going or why. When we arrived, we were placed in a camp. This camp was where the Chinese market is now, and where the former movie theatre 'October' was. We found out that some sort of government commission brought us there, and that they were re-examining our cases, and granting an amnesty to many of us.

I was one of the first. It all happened in the hall of the 'Hotel Magadan'. They brought us, 15 men, under guard into this hall. I immediately notice that behind the long table at which the presidium usually sat were all military officers of high rank – generals, and the one presiding was the highest rank.

They call my name.

They ask the first question.

"Do you consider yourself guilty of that for which you were sentenced?"

I say: "Since I was condemned, I must be guilty of something."

The colonel-general who asked this question, turns to his neighbour and comments: "See what happens, people even consider themselves to be guilty."

Then he asks me: "If we were to free you, where would you go?"

I say: "I don't know; probably nowhere. I would stay here – I'm well accustomed to this climate by now."

He listens to my answer, then speaks.

"In that case, you're rehabilitated. Sleep in the camp tonight; tomorrow you'll receive your documents. A passport will come later – you'll receive every privilege. You'll have priority for living quarters. You can visit any city. You can live in any place you choose. You'll have all the privileges of one who served in the war."

The next morning they called me and gave me a certificate indicating that on August 18th 1956, by the order of the Presidium of Supreme Soviet of the

USSR, in view of the unfounded accusations… my sentence was remitted and all rights returned. It was stamped and signed with several signatures.

I went right away to get a passport and there I met Anna, my future wife. We got acquainted.

* * * * *

The day after being freed, I was in high spirits, rejoicing that I was free, and that I was among people again. After all, only two or three months before, the thought that I might never have a family or children had shrouded my every thought. I imagined that I would leave the camps at 50 years old – and who would need me then? But there was also another warm, light-giving, thought, which, I confess, helped me: that justice ought to prevail, and in the end would.

And here at last, my hope was justified. Justice found me, and I left with clean documents.

* * * * *

Many people who I knew in the camps played a positive role in my life and even in the fate of the city. It happened that when I was freed, I met Zhenya Sokolsk, a classical boxer. He had been released from the camps just a year before me. Many gangsters had tried to recruit him into their gang. He chose another route. In those days, thieves were everywhere, preying on people in the evenings, so that people were afraid to go out on the streets. He and his friends decided to help the police catch those thieves.

They were quite successful in this. They caught many gangsters, rendering their gangs useless. They were so successful that Magadan became safe. But the gangsters decided to take revenge on him. Finally, a gang who had been threatening him caught him alone near the bus station. They attacked him. He was without a weapon, yet defended himself with his last strength. He had 17 knife wounds in him, yet as they later told, he laid up three of their men. And so he died.

* * * * *

It had been many years since I had seen my parents, but I hadn't given up hope that I would find them once more. After the death of Stalin, we had been allowed to send and receive letters from the camps. Many, especially the Ukrainians, started to write. And they began to receive packages – many which contained cured bacon. I had also started to write. No one had answered me from Xarbin – I didn't know that few were left there, that all had been exiled. I was all alone. After that I wrote to the Red Cross, and wrote to Moscow. Moscow answered that no one was living at that address and could not be found. The Red Cross never even answered.

So after I had left the camps, I carefully wrote to Xarbin again. Then I would know for sure if anyone was left there. With time, of course, I began to realise that it was very unlikely my parents were still alive. It was useless to search for them.

* * * * *

After I was freed from the camps, people in Magadan treated me normally – simply normally. I can say that I was lucky in this matter. When I applied for work at the bakery, I remember the director looked at my documents and commented aloud: "Oh, rehabilitated? We need to give you a better job."

I worked at the bakery for several months, and they chose me for the union. From the union, they sent me for further study. I enrolled in the department of journalism. I didn't continue after the first year.

The thing was that there was such strain at work, which I couldn't escape. They had made me head of the division. The bakery had a stressful production cycle, as people depended on bread to live. It was impossible to stop it for anything, one simply worked around the clock. If someone didn't show up for work, you had to find a substitute or fill in yourself. Thus I often had to run around looking for a replacement after six at night. If I didn't find anyone I had to stay and work myself till morning.

So I could not finish my journalism studies. But I still had a love for professional journalism. In 1971, I received the post of part-time correspondent for Magadan's *Pravda*. I didn't write a lot for the newspaper. I only began seriously writing in 1999, when they announced a contest for the best written story. In the first part of the year I took second place and received a prize of 350 roubles. Then in the later part of the same year, I

116

won again, first place this time and a prize of 500 roubles. And I loved to write. There was a moral stimulus, as I understood that readers appreciated the high professionalism of my stories. It meant I had to continue.

These last five years I have had over 50 stories published. If someone asked me now why I write these stories, I would answer, not only because I enjoy writing, but because I want to help my people – so that when they read my stories, they forget, for a little bit, their own problems, and maybe find a little love for one another, and all God's creation, a little more.

Probably for this reason, I meet with great interest with the pastor of the Church of the Nativity, Fr Michael. He's a good person – very sympathetic. He exudes great energy and courage. When I see him, my spirits always pick up. And it's very important that there are meetings in church for the rehabilitated victims of repression. It means a lot for them.

This is not only a person's recollections, but history.

It needs to be preserved.

Polina Vasilevna Ens

Born:	April 13th 1926
Where:	Chel'abinsk
Country:	Russia
Exiled to Germany:	1942
Deported to USSR:	1945
Imprisoned:	Archangelsk oblast, without trial or recourse
Released:	1958
Rehabilitated:	1992

I WAS BORN IN CHEL'ABINSK ON APRIL 13th 1926 to a hard-working family. We had a small farm – two horses and a cow. We were considered middle class. According to Mama, Papa worked treating leather.

In 1928 our family was forced into exile. When it became known, that Papa had a German surname – Kurtz – we were put on a list of those to be arrested. Local officials came to us one night and warned us of the danger. Without packing, my parents hitched a wagon, gathered the children, all five of us, and set off on this unavoidable flight.

Father's family was in Cuxumi in Abkhazia. So we headed there. I don't remember how long we wandered, I was still very little. When we got there we had to find somewhere to stay. There was a warehouse on the shore, where they settled migrants. There were many Russians and Germans like us among them, and so we too settled there. It wasn't complicated to get settled in – we simply hung up a sheet to separate us from the others in the warehouse!

My older brother Ivan and sister Olga helped Papa work in the village. My little sister and I guarded our things. Of the seven children born to my mother and father, two died in childhood. There were five of us still: me, Olga, Ivan, Tamara and little baby Sasha.

121

I remember Mama travelling overnight to the village on free days. She brought back apples. Papa found work pouring cement at the docks, but he and I couldn't take the ocean climate very well; we were constantly sick and suffered from boils.

So in 1935 we decided to move to Kherson in Ukraine. Things were very difficult. Papa found work at the brick factory, but with so many children it was difficult to be settled, and we were half-starving.

In order to help us even a little bit, Papa's boss took me to his *dacha* for the summer with his family – his wife and a daughter my age. We became good friends, and I was able to eat well. But mainly, we could spend the time doing interesting things. I liked being with them at the *dacha*; we swam and lay in the sun.

However one night, the boss – a grown man – tried to come on to me, but I wouldn't allow it. Not even telling anyone, I went back home. But I didn't stay there long. A woman from Kindiyki, the neighbouring village, took me as a nanny for her children. I cared for other people's children for five years, first this woman's, and then her neighbour's.

I still have a photograph with these two women in it. When it was taken all my family, who are also in it, were still alive – Papa, Mama, my brother and sisters. We took this photograph right before the beginning of the war. Really I was still a young girl when the war began. After the declaration of war in 1941, I went to work in a factory.

* * * * *

God watched over our family. Once, when they began a bombing run, Mama was feeding little Sasha. A shell fell quite close, destroying the wall next to the bed on which they were sitting.

There was a grain elevator across the road. I remember how it burnt when they bombed it, the flames reached so high. The shock wave broke a large container of sunflower oil, so that the oil poured out onto the ground. My little sister Tamara and I managed to crawl over there to gather up the oil.

The bombings continued one after the other, till we were all exhausted from them, getting practically no sleep at all. At night we all moved to shelter in the potato cellar.

When the Germans began to round up people and send them to Germany, I was among the first they captured. Mama and Papa were frantic when they found out about it and desperately tried to get me released. The first time they let me go; but in the next series of raids, not one member of our family was spared this fate. Everyone, except Papa, was exiled to Germany.

On the train carriages in which they transported prisoners was written 'sugar'. They were cattle cars. The only opening from which we could get some fresh air in these overcrowded wagons was a little vent higher than a man. I have never been able to forget this torturous trip – even though I wanted to.

* * * * *

No one in our family every found out what happened to our father. They took him away to some unknown fate.

* * * * *

The place we were sent to was called Auschwitz. They fed us undercooked potato peels, and *kasha* flavoured with a bit of sunflower oil. My family was left in this camp till the spring of 1945, when the Soviet army freed Germany.

I wasn't in the camp long. They took my sister and me to work as house servants. I was a nanny for a German family in Radobol, not far from Dresden. The very first day my boss gave me a little closet to live in, in which only my bed would fit.

My sister was taken to work for a family of wine makers in Dresden. Her boss cultivated grapes. Tamara took care of their two children.

Our city of Radobol was quite close to Dresden where my little sister was. I could even see it on the horizon out of a window in my little room. But we rarely saw each other.

From the time we arrived in Germany, I began to quickly pick up the German language. I could understand German conversation and read the newspapers and magazines a little. Even though we were German in ancestry, we had never spoken German at home.

There were regular bombings at that time. When the air-raid sirens sounded, all the members of their family went down to the basement, but I went to my room in the attic. All I could see was an enormous cloud of black smoke rising over the ruins of Dresden. It was horrible to think that somewhere in that ocean of fire was my sister. It seems there was no place for the living in that hell. There soon followed a second bombing run. The army hospital on the shore of the Elbe was destroyed.

In complete despair, and against all reason, I firmly resolved to return to Mama in the camp. They didn't want to let me go, they worried about me, but I insisted. I could only make it to the Elbe River. There were no further roads. The bridge was destroyed which led to Auschwitz and my parents.

On Sunday I headed to Dresden. I made it to where my sister had lived and worked, and found the house in ruins. I assumed that Olga had died in the bombings. It was the May 5th 1945.

Nearby, the cannonade roared on; the bombing continued. I cried from fear and sorrow till evening. A passer-by offered to help, to give me work. Someone else offered to find me shelter. I refused, with my tears showing that I only wanted to reach Mama in the camp.

Tears didn't help the situation. There was no way to get through; I had to return to the family I worked for. I was afraid – I didn't want them yelling at me.

I got to their house and simply sat with my back to the wall. A neighbour noticed me there and told them. The woman I worked for came out – I assumed to scold me. But instead of being mad at me, she hugged me, weeping with pain and joy that I returned alive and healthy. The children also rejoiced that I had come back; we hugged and cried all together.

* * * * *

Soon the Soviet army liberated this area. They were to take us Russians back to the Soviet Union. The lady tried to talk me into staying. She suggested we go to the country where no one would be looking for me.

"Get married, find work – you can live here!" She tried to convince me with tears: "Don't go!"

I couldn't imagine living so far from my homeland. I also wanted to see my parents, sisters and brother. I made the simple decision to return to Kherson.

Who would have thought that my own homeland would receive me as they did? They sentenced me to go immediately to a place not too far away, to the north Archangelsk oblast.

* * * * *

At Archangelsk was a German colony. Everyone who returned from Germany was forced to live together. They put us in a prison camp in three barracks. The living conditions began to improve only toward the end of the '50s when they started to put people in individual huts. But before that they took me to Onegu in the Archangelsk oblast. In 1947 I was moved to Topivo, to the Karelsk lumber station. I worked there processing timber.

At first I worked on cut logs, slicing and hauling them myself. We had to trim the branch stubs by hand to smooth the log, and so were constantly tearing our gloves and never able to mend them. It was very labour intensive, difficult work, which seriously affected my health. Later I had to acclimatise to work under the supervisor.

We didn't work under guard. Of course, they weren't needed. The winters were long and severe with freezing cold weather; we were miles from the next village, and inadequately dressed for such conditions – no wonder we never went far. And even if someone dared try to escape, there were packs of wolves which would eat you.

Twenty kilometres from Topiva, and 40 kilometres from Onegi, was the village of Chekuevo. There they sent us girls in the summer, in pairs or teams of three to cut wood. We had to cut down large, old, gnarled trees with bow saws.

I remember that on our team was a tall, affable, interesting gal – Milya Saprykina. We went to our designated tree, we looked at it… And we nearly cried from weakness. Only God knows what a miracle it was for us young, half starved girls to manage to tackle such huge trees – we practically did it all by hand.

But this world is not without good people. They could be found even in this God-forsaken place. The brigade leader and commandant helped us a lot. Not always, of course, but they often helped us. Milya was older than I, sociable. So they liked to have a smoke and talk with us on our short breaks – now we had someone to complain to, and pour out our pain. They listened with sympathy and feeling and helped us. It's hard to overestimate the value of their help and what it meant to us. Thanks to their attention, we were able to survive.

They gave us 2.2 pounds of bread a day. If we didn't fulfil our quota, they reduced our ration to 21 ounces. When the only other food they gave us was oats with mushrooms, then the only substantial food we had was bread. And if they cut our ration of bread, we no longer had the strength to do hard physical labour.

Often the brigade leader and commandant help us to fulfil our quota – which was no less than 176.5 cubic feet of lumber. In thanks we cried to God and prayed that He would protect them and keep them healthy. God protected them and us.

Once a tree fell on me, and I was very seriously injured by the branches. It was a miracle that I wasn't killed. I lay in the hospital for a long time, and then when I was released, I had to walk 40 kilometres all night to the mill. They put me on lighter work. I carried logs after that.

* * * * *

From the mill to the loading point was eight kilometres. In the winter we hauled the logs on sleds, and in the summer on trolleys, to the loading point. Usually they would build barracks there in the woods close to where we worked. We lived in these barracks – if you can call it living – unfinished buildings that were dirty and crawling with cockroaches. I would come in deathly tired after working, fall down to sleep and the cockroaches wouldn't give me any rest. I would sleep and they would crawl over my body. It's terrible even to describe it. There were no sanitary facilities; the whole place was rancid. But we slept in these barracks; and in the morning we went off to work in the lumber mill.

Of course, we were rarely there. We worked all day, from sunrise till sunset. It was particularly difficult with the arctic days, when the sun didn't go below the horizon. It seemed as if the unbelievably hard work would never end.

I only ever left that place when the horse needed to be re-shod. I went to Topivo. Only then could I allow myself to meet with Dima, with whom my fate was wound. This gentleman became a part of my life.

* * * * *

In 1947 when I came here Dima was only 21years old. He worked as a blacksmith, and lived in an apartment of a female acquaintance by the name of Katherine. Whenever I was in town, I usually stopped by her place. Once I asked her to buy potatoes for me in the village. The next time, I went by to get my potatoes with the intention of returning to the mill. She told me about her boarder.

The men had a higher quota to fill than we did. Dima's health didn't leave him the strength to fulfil the quota. They cut his bread rations down to 28 ounces a day. He was trapped in a circle. Under such great physical duress, a young man's body needed good food.

When I found out about his condition, I asked her to give him one of my potatoes. That served as an excuse for getting to know each other better. We found out that we had a lot in common. We had both experienced the loss of close friends and family. Both he and I had already lost our fathers.

In 1950, Dima proposed, and we got married. We had a son, Ivan and a daughter Anna. I now already have grown-up grandchildren.

* * * * *

After the death of Stalin, life got a little better. The food ration was increased, and in the kiosks there appeared 'edible' food and macaroni. We were allowed to buy 17 ounces of sugar or caramel bon-bons on our ration cards.

Only after my daughter was born in 1954 was I permitted to stop going to work. By then, I had slaved for eight years at that lumber mill.

They released us in 1958, but they didn't give us passports. It was impossible to leave. On May 28th 1958, we moved to Onegi. My husband worked and I began sewing at home. I cut out the patterns and sewed gym suits and trousers. Little by little we made a life. We got several domestic animals – two goats and some chickens. The choice of animals wasn't accidental. After the camps, my husband was left with an open wound, known as a fistula. The application of goat's milk helped him heal. It was good for the children as well.

They started to ask me to sew one thing and another. One woman asked me to sew a jacket for her. Even though I hadn't really sewed anything so complicated, the jacket came out well. We started to talk. It turned out that the husband of this woman was also arrested at the end of the '30s and sentenced to 10 years without correspondence. She was left with two children. She told me she had written an impassioned letter asking whether they could at least correspond. She had received permission.

This inspired us to look for my brother Ivan and other relatives. I was illiterate, and so this kind woman wrote a request in my name for information on the fates of our relatives. In answer we received a letter in which we found out that my brother Ivan was here in a camp in Magadan. We found out that Mama had been able to return for a little while to Kherson after Auschwitz, but they soon deported her to Siberia, too.

My husband insisted we should go to them. We gave our farm animals, our goat and all our 'wealth' to his fellow worker, Leonid. We went to Mama near Novosibirsk. She was living in Iskitim. My sister and brother lived near her. Of course, she wanted us to live nearby too, so that all her children would be close by. She worked at a cement factory in those days.

We travelled and met with everyone that I thought I had lost for ever. It turned out that Olga, my little sister whom I had thought was killed in the bombing of Dresden, had lived with her husband for a long time not far from Onegi. They were in the Archangelsk oblast, no more than 800 kilometres from us, and we had never known!

We lived with Mama for about a month. The family was huge – 13 people. It was very crowded, with Olga's four children and our family. My children had to sleep under the beds, as there was no place else to sleep.

Then we received a message from my husband's brother. He invited us to come to Magadan, even offering to help with expenses for a time. This led

The remains of a camp in Butugichag mountains, where prisoners were sent to work in uranium and tin mines.

Buildings like this housed inmates at the uranium and tin mines at Butugichag.

Above: The remains of a building high in the Butugichag mountains, home to thousands of the 'repressed' during Stalin's oppressive regime.
Below: The mountains of Butugichag still bear the scars of the uranium mines, where thousands of the 'repressed' were put to work in terrible conditions.

The remains of a solitary confinement cell in the Butugichag mountain camp.

Above: The 'Mask of Sorrows' memorial to the 'repressed', Magadan.
Below: Garlands decorate a weeping figure at the 'Mask of Sorrows' memorial.

The Crucifix at the 'Mask of Sorrows' memorial.

Stones at the 'Mask of Sorrows' memorial bear the symbols of the religions of those who lost their lives or suffered horrific treatment in the gulag prison camps.

Stones at the 'Mask of Sorrows' memorial bear the symbols of the religions of those who lost their lives or suffered horrific treatment in the gulag prison camps.

Stones at the 'Mask of Sorrows' memorial bear the symbols of the religions of those who lost their lives or suffered horrific treatment in the gulag prison camps.

Markers at the 'Mask of Sorrows' memorial bear the names of the major prison camps in the Kolyma region.

Above: Serpentina, an execution camp built on a winding road like a snake; thus the camp was named 'Serpentine' after the terrain. When the prisoners were taken down this road they knew by the winding of it that it was leading to their deaths. **Below:** Maglag

Markers at the 'Mask of Sorrows' memorial bear the names of the major prison camps in the Kolyma region.

Above: Kendjal

Below: Heneekandja and, in the background, Butugichag, a camp where prisoners mined uranium ore. To work there was almost a death sentence because the ore was processed without any protection. The prisoners would constantly breathe the dust, and many died within months of going there.

Above: The 'Mask of Sorrows' memorial looks over the snow-covered hills around Magadan.

Below: Survivors make their way through blizzard conditions to climb the 'Mask of Sorrows' memorial during a service commemorating those who died in the prison camps.

The beautiful forests of Siberia. Many prisoners lost their lives here, either as a result of the freezing weather or in tree-felling accidents.

Above: A cross with a simple inscription marks the site of a mass grave where hundreds of victims are buried.
Below: Prayers at the site of the mass grave.

Above: The site of an unmarked mass grave where hundreds of victims of the camps lie buried.
Below: Looking town on the town of Magadan from the surrounding hills.

The Cross at the site of hundreds of unmarked graves carries the words: "In this unmarked grave our lives have ended. Who could forget about us if he is a human being?"

us to move here in 1959. I'll always remember how difficult this trip was. We declined monetary help from our relatives.

From Iskitim to Novosibirsk, we travelled on a train, then by plane. There was only a little air transportation at that time. The distances were great. We bought some tea for the children on the road, and added a piece of bread to the tea. That was our simple meal for the kids. We had to go without food.

We arrived in Magadan, hungry, weak and dirty.

* * * * *

My husband's brother met us. At first we lived with him in his room. He worked at that time as a plasterer-cum-painter. The first buildings of Magadan, on Lenin Street, bear the results of his labours.

My husband found work as a blacksmith. For six months we rented some rooms in a private home. They helped us find a day nursery for the children. I found work as a technical worker in a grocery store; then they put me in a dish shop on Parkovia Street. I always worked conscientiously, and my duties included helping the delivery people. However the delivery men were often drunk, and then I had to unload everything myself. Now I can't even imagine how that worked out. From there I went to the furniture store on Parkovia Street, and then they sent me to the 'House of Clothing'.

Life was always difficult; it seems at times that we never lived, but just survived. We worked all our lives at hard work. In 1977, my husband and I retired.

I had a happy marriage with Dima. He died three months short of our 55th anniversary. We experienced many losses together, endured many sorrows. But because we knew the heavy burden of such difficulties, we lived very closely, valuing, protecting and caring for each other.

* * * * *

In those unfinished camp settlements, the one freedom we had was prayer to God. Nothing was worse than uncertainty. By whose evil will did we receive such a fate? Why did we suffer so without cause? There was no trial. What could be more horrible than innocent imprisonment? We were like the damned and the cursed: exiled and forced to survive the permafrost in the forest, surrounded by silence and oblivion.

The mark of a prisoner has been on me all my life. I conscientiously fulfilled the most difficult, the most thankless, jobs; I couldn't allow myself to work poorly. I'm a reliable person. People saw that, and respected me. Yet no matter how conscientiously I worked, I never received any encouragement, no premium, nor any nice present, like other workers. The one reward was a badge: "I'm a 'German', and was in Germany."

This fact played a decisive role in my life story. I was sent there through no fault of my own and I often have mourned this fact. In Germany, I suffered because I was from Russia, and in Russia I suffered all my life because I was 'German'.

All my remaining life after the camps, I never rid myself of the stigma of being a German. Its persistent weight was present everywhere. Many people who just happened to cross our paths, at work or in public, let it be known by words and actions that we were different. They wouldn't let us forget that we were 'Germans' and prisoners.

Only faith in God helped. I'm baptised. I learned my prayers in childhood. But at difficult times, in the camps and at dangerous moments, the prayers were expressed naturally. If it wasn't for my faith, I would have died long ago. How many times we begged God for death, so as to be finished with the burden of hunger, cold, and tiredness! We came home late after work. Our cotton trousers would barely dry from the snow in the short hours of rest at night. In the morning we put on damp clothes and again went into the cold. In such situations, it's difficult to imagine anything except faith that could help one endure such difficulties.

Not long before my husband's death, his family sent us a children's Bible. We have a real Psalter, the New Testament, and a Bible. I read them all. The words give comfort. It's too bad my sight is now poor. I hope my grandchildren will read them.

It was very difficult to endure the loss of my husband. He died three months short of his 78th birthday. It's very difficult living without him.

But when I read the Word of God, I feel better.

And I always look forward to the meetings with the rehabilitated, which the Church of the Nativity hosts for us. We need them so very much.

Sofia Ivanovna Kononenko

Born:	September 29th 1924
Where:	Lishnia, Buchach Region, Ternopilskaia Oblast
Country:	Ukraine
Arrested:	1947
Sentence:	10 years of corrective labour camp
Released:	1955
Rehabilitated:	1991

I WAS BORN INTO A PEASANT FAMILY. There were six children, five brothers and me. We lived under Polish rule. I went to Polish schools. I finished six years of schooling.

Our family were farmers. We had our own field, our own horses, our own cows, pigs, chickens and geese. Back then everyone in the village had their own farms. This was how we made our living.

There was a lot of work. At night I herded the cattle. I would return, and everyone would be sleeping. There was no light. I could also ride a horse. I worked for my papa like a man. I ploughed and sowed. My neighbours said to my Mama: "Maria, why do you allow her to work so? She could overstrain herself from such labour." But my Mama said: "What can I do? She wants to help us do everything."

Mama and Papa loved us children very much. They never did anyone any harm. We lived very peaceably among ourselves. Papa was an engineer on the river. He could build bridges. Our Papa was literate, Mama was illiterate. We all went to church. I remember well how we all dressed up and went to church at Easter. At Easter we all had to wear something new, even if it was just something simple. And Papa checked how everyone was dressed and whether our shoes had been polished or not. Our family was very close.

Every day we prayed, both in the morning and in the evening – the Our Father and the Hail Mary. Their images were in our small hut and we would pray. Mama told us: "See the icons, see? They tell me all about you. They tell me everything." In school we had a religion class, every day for one hour. The priest – he was the only one for three villages – would come and we prayed. Then he taught the class. He taught beautifully. He told us a great deal about Jesus Christ. He baptised me. He performed my wedding nuptials.

Then the war began. I lived with my family until I married. In 1943, right after New Year, I married. I lived with my husband until 1944, when the German occupiers began to take people away to Germany. Many – oh so many! – were driven away. My husband and I were sent to Germany. My husband's train left for Germany, but our group fell under fire and we did not go anywhere. And so we remained on our own territory. We stood. We waited. And I returned home.

At home I worked. I went back to helping on the farm. We had our own field. No one had yet taken it away. We tilled on horses. We worked with a plough. I sowed the grain myself. I was small, fragile and thin, but nevertheless I did it all. Ah, what else could I do?

In 1946 my brother Vasiliy was killed. The *Banderovtsi*, a group of Ukrainian nationalists, began to commit excesses. We were afraid of everyone. One group would come at night, they would take the horses. Others would come during the day: "Come on, hand over the milk, eggs, bread." We did not know who to trust and who to fear. They would come at night dressed in military uniforms and speak Russian. Others came during the day: "Give us the milk can – we need milk." And you had to hand it over. You had to give up your eggs. That was how it was. Back then they levied very large taxes on everyone.

Then the *Banderovtsi* killed Papa, because he refused to help them. They came to my father and said: "You should defend our families. If the Russians come, you should inform us."

My father said: "I'll be killed by you or sent to prison by them. I do not know which to choose. I do not want either."
They came at night. They took Papa away. We cried with Mama. They shot our dog. Papa was taken to the woods and killed there. And then one villager told us how these people who killed Papa also perished the next

day. They too were killed. That is how my father died, so we do not even know where his grave is.

* * * * *

In 1947, I was arrested. They said that my husband was in a gang. I told them that in 1944 we were taken together to Germany, not only us, but many people. They didn't believe me. They demanded my documents from me. What could I show? I had no letter, no documents at all.

I was kept under arrest by the NKVD for a whole year.

More than 40 people sat in one cell. The *parasha*, a large chamber pot, stood in the corner where we could go according to our needs. We covered our faces from the stench with a scarf or something else. We were given food to eat twice a day and were led outside for five minutes. A year passed. I was summoned. And without a trial or an investigation, my sentence was read – 10 years in corrective labour camps. They sentenced me on two counts: Article 54 and Article 58. I did not sign anything – not the court decision or anything else. After this I was taken away to Lviv. From there we were taken by train to Taishet in the Irkutsk oblast to cut timber.

In Taishet we cut tree trunks and put them in the Chinar River. The trunks floated further down the river. Down the river was the men's camp. These prisoners caught the trees and hauled them to wherever they needed to go.

In camp I wore a number. I did not say my surname, but only called out my number: D-2151. The number was on my hat on my head. The number was on the knee on the trouser leg of my cotton trousers. The same number was on the shoulder. It was written on a white rag in large blue letters: D-2151. I called out this number.

After Taishet, we were taken to Vanino Bay. They put us with common criminals – thieves, rapists and other dishonourable people. Those sentenced for ordinary, everyday crimes attacked us. They took away all of our belongings. I had beautiful, red boots. I had taken them with me from Ukraine. They were taken away from me. I remained barefoot. They took my beautiful woollen scarf.

There was a woman, Kharlamova, who is with us here in Magadan. She worked as a radio announcer. She worked there for a long time and then left. And she served out her sentence at the same time together with me. She was the one who stood up for me. She told these wenches: "At least bring back the boots." They brought the boots back.

A fight took place there, at Vanino Bay. The prisoners who were serving time under Article 58 got into a bloody fight with those prisoners who were serving time for ordinary crimes, because they wouldn't give us shelter. Then a large group of soldiers herded us out and led us, the political prisoners, away. We were taken away to a big field and sat down on the ground. After this we began to be sent to assigned places.

* * * * *

I was brought to Magadan on the ship *Miklukha Maklai*. Convoy guards met us. We were put into columns of five and led off. They brought us here as a labour force. There was no one there but men, only men, both free workers and former prisoners who had been brought here earlier. There were many men. And when our columns of women came from the port, the men threw money at our feet. They earned money at the mines. They had not seen a woman's face for many years.

We were led from the port to a camp where the macaroni factory is now. There were barracks there. We were driven into the barracks. The *parasha* was put in and we were given nothing to eat all day. Only towards evening was a dry ration brought in.

The next day we were sent on farther by transport. I ended up in the camp at the 15 kilometre mark. I worked there for some time at the brick factory. We moulded and baked bricks.
For half a year I worked cutting timber. We cut wood for the wooden homes that stand here in Magadan. We walked for miles on foot, with the saw on our backs, the axe in our hands. We would go to an area of wooded land and choose a tree. First, you hew the trunk, and then you cut. Then you break off the branches and twigs. After this, you measure – you needed 40 and 20 foot lengths. You measure and then cut with your saw. After this the prepared log was rolled down.

There was a lot of hard, backbreaking work, yet the nourishment was meagre – almost nothing. It reached the point that we would walk to cut timber and I would have to stop and rest. I could not walk. The supervisors did not see that I was already yellow, that my eyes were already yellow. It

136

was not visible to them. In the morning I was herded out, at night herded in. I had no strength to move. I had fallen ill with Hepatitis A.

Our brigade leader was a girl from Lviv. She had gone to the boss and said: "I will not take Kravchuk, because she cannot walk. She is sick. I do not want the whole brigade to fall behind because of her." If the quota was not fulfilled, then the food rations were cut. They said that I should go to the medical point. The doctor looked at my eyes. I looked here and there, but by now my whole body was yellow. Up until then I had never been sick, but now I had Hepatitis!

I had gone to the medical point by myself. There was a hospital with five beds. I was carried there on a stretcher. I could not walk by myself. They stuck needles in me, treated me and then they cancelled everything. They gave me only *kasha* – oats and barley, oats and barley, and that was it. But the girls ate different food. In the mess hall there was fish, fried fish. In the second half of the summer in Magadan there was a lot of fish. When fish spawn in the creek, then thousands of fish are lying there. Take as much as you want and eat them. We roasted fish on a fire! You cannot imagine how delicious it was! We made skewers from wooden twigs and roasted it on the fire, and then ate it.

The girls in the hospital also ate fish. How I wanted fish after all this *kasha*! How I wanted it! I got up at night. I went to the mess hall. This fish, covered with a napkin, was there on a little table. I stole a piece of the fish. They were all sleeping in one room. I went into another. And there was still a piece of garlic there. I ate all this with such pleasure, but in the morning I had a fever. The next day I was asked: "What did you eat?" Everyone posed this question to me. And I said that I had stolen the fish from the girls and eaten it.

"Well, now you won't be getting out of here," they told me.

There was a Marika Kovalchuk from Lviv in the camp. She came to me and said: "Sonia, you are seriously ill." She loved me very much. We even slept next to each other. Marika said: "You need to heal." She went to the barracks to look for lice. Six live lice were needed, and she found them. She gathered the lice in a jar, alive. And then she made little flat cakes. She baked them and in each she put a live louse. She brought them and sat near me and put each in my mouth. And I, stupidly, did not know anything. She put the flat cakes in my mouth so that I did not bite them with my teeth, but swallowed. I swallowed them as she said. One was gone and then another. I swallowed six. After this, the Hepatitis A disappeared. So I had recovered from Hepatitis A and was no longer sick. Many years have passed since I received my freedom, but I do not feel as though my liver was ever ill. That is how Marika Kovalchuk cured me.

* * * * *

In the beginning we lived in a tent. Five iron barrels were put in it. They were fuelled with some combustible material. We settled down on two-level bunks. Here my two boards lay, there another's two boards, and a third person's two boards. No-one had the right to sit on another's board. I was on the top. Like everyone, I tried to 'catch' the warmth. You put your head toward the fire – you would warm up, but your legs would freeze. If you put your head to the wall, then your legs would be warm, but your head would freeze.

We lay down to sleep in our jerseys, in padded cotton trousers, and in felt boots. How we came in from work is how we laid down to sleep. No one undressed. I had a cotton blanket, a cotton pillow, and mattress. And I slept on this. I had no sheets. We were given clothes – old black skirts and jackets that were also black or dark blue. The pillow cases that we were given for our pillow were also dark blue. I ate half a ration of bread. I worked at the bakery. I left half for the next day. And so I collected a ration of bread. After two days I could exchange it for two pillow cases from the men and sew myself a blouse from these pillow cases. It was beautiful, a blue sateen blouse with sleeves. All of us girls knew how to sew and embroider. We did not have much light, just a few small oil lamps. In the evening we lit tiny pieces of iron. We sat near them. We made everything that we needed. We could embroider around this light.

I cut up various pieces of rags and sewed a blanket. I made a cotton pillow. I embroidered for myself, for prisoners, and for free workers. They would bring me sugar in exchange for this. This sugar helped me to avoid exhaustion. There were some girls who had support. Packages were sent to them. They were sent lard, dried bagels. But I did not have anything except my prison rations. Nothing else. When I began to sew these beautiful pillow cases, then the free workers began to place orders: sew this, sew that. They began to bring me sugar and sometimes even a piece of butter.

They brought me thread. I embroidered day and night. I did not think about how I was sitting in a prison. I would just come back from work and would embroider. It was easier that way to endure all the burdens, keeping yourself busy with work. After work, like usual, we went to the mess hall. We ate soup or were given something else, and that was all. We went to the barracks and began to work on our projects.

There were no days off. True, when there were big holidays, Easter or Christmas, we managed to celebrate, nevertheless. The Lithuanians freed us up when it was our Easter. When they celebrated Easter, we worked for them and they sat in the barrack and celebrated. And so we cooperated and were friends among ourselves.

* * * * *

In 1952 our numbers were removed from us. During the years that I was in prison, we were often "thrown about," as they would say, to fill holes if there was a place where a labour force was needed. We were taken from the camp and transported to that place. I cut hay at the 47th kilometre. Once we were even brought to the mine called Matrosov. We were there for just three days. We collected little stones in the stream. We found beautiful, glimmering stones. We brought them home. How were we to know that this was gold?! We took them with us. And then the geologists came. They took these stones from us. They said it was gold. But who among us could have known it was gold – shiny stones, that's all!

* * * * *

On the day Stalin died, they did not make us work. No one worked. Everyone was kept inside the barracks. All the guards came and observed how each of us conducted herself. Twice security officers came to question me. Why didn't I cry? I asked him how could I cry for Stalin? After all I was raised under Polish rule. I do not know for whom I would cry. Probably I would only cry for my parents, but not for anyone else. When the horn of the steam ships began to sound, we all dropped to the ground. We didn't go to work the next day. We sat in the barracks.

* * * * *

After Stalin's death, in 1954 to be more precise, I began to work as a cook. At that time a children's home was started at the 15th kilometre. It was a large home and the children of the women prisoners were kept there. While the women served in the camps, their children where in this children's home. The military was constantly checking it. The children were cared for there until they were three years old. After three they were taken to Khabarovsk, to Kazan and to other cities on the mainland. A very small plane flew from the 13th kilometre. The children were taken and two escorts flew with them. Just 28 people. And then the children's home was closed and we were brought to Snezhnaia Dolina.

The head of this house brought me to work with her. I ended up working in the bakery. Olga Smolenskaia was the head baker. Three of us worked there. Every day I was given a ration of bread. But those who worked in the bakery did not eat this ration of bread. Every day I gave this ration to the brigade, and from there it was distributed to each prisoner in turn. How many there were then in the camp! Today this one receives two rations, then another receives two rations, and so on, in turn. The whole brigade receives my ration in turn.

I remember well this ration of bread in Irkutsk. You would get it and put it under your pillow. You'd lie there and think: "I will only pinch off a little." You pinch, you eat. You pinch, you eat. Then you lift up your pillow and you have nothing left there. You have already eaten it all, but the whole day lies ahead.

I remember one incident with bread, which happened in our camp. The rations of bread, which were given to us, were cut and weighed. If, let's suppose, it was a third of an ounce short, a little piece of bread was cut and stuck into the top of the ration with a little wooden stick.

A woman from our brigade was chosen to pick up the bread. She went to the bakery. She got the bread and carried it back, but she took all these pieces used to make up the weight from the ration. When the brigade learned about this, the girls almost killed her. At first they accused her, but then decided to check. She went out for something. They went to her bed, lifted her pillow, and it was all there under her pillow, all these pieces of bread used to make the weight. Then they asked her: "Do you want more?"

She said: "I don't." It's true, she then fell on her knees crying, and asked for forgiveness. She said: "I won't eat my ration for several days in order to compensate for the small pieces that I took."

* * * * *

Before my arrest I had taken cookery courses. A young girl from Kiev came to us and taught us. After this my mother-in-law said: "My daughter-in-law can boil potatoes so that they will be delicious without lard, without butter. It will be delicious, because she finished a course." And therefore I was taken to work as a cook. The girls went to the forest, but I remained to work as a cook.

The mess hall was not very big. People would just arrive, eat, and then a second group would arrive. That was a special assignment. The administrators never had any grievances against me, although anything could happen.

Once I needed to stoke the stove, but there was no wood. I was still not a free worker. I had not been released. I could not go outside the zone. The guard sat there. He would not allow me out to get firewood. "It's not allowed," he said. So I took an axe and cut down the door of the old toilet. I carried the wood inside, stoked the stove, and prepared everything.

The boss comes and says: "What are we going to do with you?"

I reply: "Whatever you want to do, do. But what do you think would happen if people came back from such work to eat, and I have nothing prepared for them? You can eat at home. You can buy yourself a piece of bread, but they cannot buy anything."

He looks intensely at me but says nothing.

People say later that he said: "Well, she's a hero."

* * * * *

I was released in 1955. I remember that the head of the camp brought me to Magadan with him and I received my work book. I was now a free worker. I was told: "Sofia Ivanovna, don't go home yet. Work three years, you'll receive some money. Then you can go and have a look. Since the war, it is hard to live there. It's poor. They live very poorly."

When I was in camps, I wrote letters to my family twice a year. More than that was not allowed. After I left the camps, I could write as much as I wanted. And I knew that Mama was living very poorly. In one year Mama had to live through three deaths in the family. It was very hard on her.

After the war, it was very hard in general. Papa was gone. There was no one to help her on the farm. My two brothers, her two sons, Mikhail and Leonid, remained with her. Of course, they worked. They helped her as they could. But it was very difficult to find a job. They went to the forest and gathered wild strawberries and sold them, just to survive.

After my release, I started to work and earn money. I received my first payment of 800 roubles and gave it to a woman who lived there in the city of Magadan. She sent the money to my Mama. Mama received the money and did not know how to react. She was so happy she cried for joy.

Everyone in the village envied her that she had received so much money. When Mama received the notice, she could not read it; she was illiterate. Her sons were not home. Mikhail was gathering wild strawberries in the woods. He came back from the woods, and Mama gave him the notice. "You know, I found this little paper in the garden." He read it and jumped for joy. He said: "Mama, now you can buy me a suit. Oh, how we will live!" They were so filled with joy over this money I sent! She bought a calf. She bought seeds for the garden – everything that was necessary for the farm.

Mama wrote me a letter later. She asked: "You probably have no dress." In fact, I was without a dress, without a coat. I only ate. Everything that I received, I sent off to her. But I was satisfied that I had done something good for my mother. My poor Mama had suffered so much.

* * * * *

Before my release, I met a young man at Snezhnaia Dolina, who then became my second husband. He was also one of those repressed. He had been in the war. He flew on a small reconnaissance plane. He photographed German warehouses and bases. Everything on the front was very strict back then. An ampoule with poison was sewn into the collar of the soldier's shirt in case of unforeseen circumstances. If the plane was brought down, he was to take the poison so as not to fall alive into the hands of the enemy. But before this, he was supposed to find a way to burn the film.

142

And this happened to him. They flew on a mission and the plane was shot down. He managed to burn the film, but he did not manage to chew the ampoule. His plane fell and he suffered concussion. He was treated in a hospital. He was cured. And then he was sentenced to execution.

He sat in prison for 40 days. He awaited his execution. This is how he told it. And there was an old man in the prison who also had been sentenced to death. The old man, before he went to his execution, told my future husband: "Vladimir, you won't go to your death. They will give you time in a camp instead." Indeed, his execution was changed to a 25-year sentence.

Then he served his sentence in the city of Komsomolsk-on-Amur in the Soviet harbour. He built the road. Soon a communication was sent to him about a change in his punishment. The article was changed and he was given only 10 years. After this he was brought here to Magadan.

We met, but I did not want to marry him, because I hoped to find my first husband. I waited for any news from him. But then I agreed. We began to live in a civil marriage. I became pregnant and in 1957, I gave birth to my child. I was 33 years old. I could not wait any longer.

I had just given birth to my child, when I received three letters from London, from my first husband!

And then: "Cry, don't cry, do what you want." My second, common law husband, of course, was severely upset. But I said: "Don't worry. Since everything has turned out this way, such is our fate. I am not going anywhere. I will live here."

My first husband had searched for me abroad. He knew that I too had been taken to Germany. But he could not find me. He started to look here, throughout all the Soviet Union and all Ukraine. He found me in Magadan only after Mama gave him my address.

What is interesting is that all this time I remembered a dream that I had in prison. This dream was about my first husband. I dreamt that I was in prison like it was today.

Every evening we pray. No matter how many people are there in prison, everyone prays. Everyone prays and then lies down to sleep.

When I lie down to sleep, this dream comes.

My husband gives me seven apples and says: "Eat these seven apples and then you will leave this hole."

Indeed, that happened. I sat in prison for seven years, but had been sentenced to 10. There you have the seven apples that he gave me.

My first husband persistently asked me to come to him in London. He asked me to travel to Poland. "Leave your child with her father and come by yourself." And he would arrive from London to get me.

What kind of mother, having given birth at the age of 33, could leave her own child? Such a mother can only be called a cuckoo. I did not go. I remained here. I lived with this husband. He worked in communications. And I worked in Day Care centre number 48, where School number two and the meteorological service are now. I worked there in this day care centre as a cook for 35 years. And so, we lived.

* * * * *

In 1991 I was rehabilitated. I was given permission to go wherever I wanted; I could even return to my homeland. But why would I return to my homeland now? By then who of mine still remained there?

After my first husband sent me the three letters, we began corresponding. Then we stopped. Then we started again. He travelled to Ternopil in Ukraine. All of his relatives went to meet him. He asked: "Why didn't you bring my wife to me?" They said that I lived in Magadan now; that I was married. "Well, so she is married," he remarked. "Let her come. I would like to see her."

After this he wrote to me: "Come alone to Kiev. You will stay in a hotel." Many years passed before he and I met again. It happened in 1981. My husband with whom I lived in Magadan was still alive. He died in 1986.
We had a very good meeting, my first husband and I. We told each other everything. He said he could not come here. He had a daughter in England. He didn't have a wife, but he had a daughter. Her name is Angela. She lives in her house and he lives in his. They go to visit each other's house as guests for dinner, usually on Sunday. Angela has two children.

In 1999 a visa came for me from England. My daughter, my granddaughter and I went to London. We went and visited there for a month. Of course, he really tried. He took us all around in his car. He showed us the kingdom, the museums. We stayed on the upper floor of a two-storey house. He slept below.

That's how I saw London. But no desire to live in London arose in me. I looked around. It is beautiful, but, nevertheless, it is not ours. And I told him this. My daughter very much wanted to stay there so that her daughter could marry there and they would resettle. I said: "No, for me there is no city better than Magadan." It has become my second homeland. Ukraine is good, but for me the very best place is here in Magadan.

Since I met with my first husband, everything in my life has come together. It was not my fault. Up until then I still believed that I was married to one husband and before God I had one husband. I was not even registered with the second. But my children are from my second husband – that's how it came together in life. You yourself could never think this up, but fate orders it so, or someone orders your fate. My first husband lived in England for 56 years.

I remember when I gave birth to my daughter. I received three letters from him. Then a package arrived from London, a 44 pound package! In it there was everything for a small baby, everything from little sandals and slippers to underwear. He sent 18 dresses and pinned to each one was a little pair of matching panties. Such attention was so touching.

* * * * *

If you talk about the treatment of those who were repressed and rehabilitated, it was not always the same. In those years many groceries were available only in limited quantities. We stood in line for several hours in order to buy a couple of pounds of oranges or mandarins. And you stand in line and sometimes you carry on a conversation. I have a Ukrainian accent. Someone begins to shout: "You *Banderovets* need to be exiled from here!"

These words were very offensive. But over time, I began to give a rebuff. I reacted aggressively. I answered: "We were brought here without respect and with a convoy guard, but you came for money, because you didn't want to work there. You thought manna would fall on you here."

I did not curse. I answered calmly. They immediately fell silent. That was it. No one said a word in response to my words. I continued to stand in this line. I am not one to be shy. I said it, bought what I needed to, and left.

But other people treated us very well. They befriended us and did not treat us with derision because we had been in prison.

I go to the meetings for those who were repressed with pleasure. In general, I like to go to the Church of the Nativity of Jesus Church. The pastor of the church, Fr Michael, is the kindest person I know. He has a good humane soul. All the parishioners notice this. When I go to church I am in a good mood. I take a candle and throw in coins. I contribute my mite, because that is how it should be. Every person should realise this.

I pray by myself with my whole heart. I pray for the souls of the deceased. I pray for my health. I pray for everything.

Ivanna Petrovna Lebedinskaia

Born:	December 23rd 1923
Where:	P'ianovichi, Samborskii region, L'vivskaia Oblast
Country:	Ukraine
Arrested:	November 20th 1945
Sentence:	10 years corrective labour, plus 5 years loss of political and civil rights.
Released:	November 20th 1954
Rehabilitated:	1986

I WAS BORN AND RAISED IN A RELIGIOUS FAMILY. My parents were believers, Greek Catholics. In western Ukraine there were almost no Orthodox. We went to church, to a Catholic church. My whole life we only knew this way. In the city there may have been a handful of atheists, but where we lived everyone was a deep believer. And everyone respected one another. My parents worked their own farm. When the Soviet power invaded and began to form collective farms, we did not join.

I was arrested on November 20th 1945. I was at home when they came and took me away. I was 22 years old. Back then everyone was accused of being involved in Ukrainian nationalist organisations. They made various other charges which were all rubbish. None of it was true. We were not mixed up in any such organisation.

The first time I was taken, I was kept in a basement. Back then there were still no plumbing pipes in basements. Instead, there were special gullies through which sewage flowed. This was our prison cell. I remember we could see the pigs which they kept in the courtyard walk by through a little window.

One grandmother was brought in, probably as old as I am now, maybe even older. The locks of her hair were braided. It seems that she had rubbed them with something and a rat gnawed off one of her braids.

The bunks were low and there were eight people in a row on them. The rats roamed freely wherever they wanted. And sewage floated by. The horror! It was frightening.

I sat there for two months and was then sent home. But within two months I was arrested a second time. The first time was some time in the summer, and the second time it was autumn, November 20th.

* * * * *

I was the only one from my family arrested, but five people were taken from our village. We were brought to the NKVD in the city of Sambor. Then we were transferred to Drogobich – this was the administrative centre. The investigation lasted three months. It was quick.

Then I was sent to Brigidka, another prison in the Drogobichskaia oblast. This was a terrible prison. Everyone who had been sentenced was sent there. I had immediately been given 10 years, plus five years loss of political and civil rights. Later, here in Magadan, I was given another two and a half years of exile.

From Drogobich, I ended up at a transit camp in Lviv. A transport was organised there and we were sent all the way to the Bay of Nakhodka. We were loaded aboard the ship *Sovietskaia Latvia*, bound for Magadan. We were tossed about at sea for almost a month. This was in the spring of 1946. We arrived in Magadan on July 2nd and my northern epic began.

We were not at the transit camp here for long. They soon settled us in the Japanese prisoner of war camp. Then they began to deliver people to different spots. I ended up cutting timber on the *trassa*, the long road leading into the interior.

I cut timber at the 23rd kilometre mark outside Magadan, and then around the 30th kilometre mark, deep in the forest on the right hand side of the road. Something had not worked out there the first time and so people had been divided up and taken away, some here and some there.

The forest was bare and cold. When we went into it, we felt such despair. "Lord, at least let a log fall on me." We wanted even this. We didn't want to live even though we were young. It was very difficult.

I worked until the autumn cutting timber. After this I was taken away to the village of Balagannoe to clean fish at the fish processing plant. The fishermen caught the fish, transported them, and threw them down in a vat. We stood in the water wearing the same clothes we walked to work in. There was nothing else, no special clothing. And we packed the fish. We were given special cases. We had to pack 1,000 Siberian salmon fish hearts in them. That was our daily routine, and for it we received a 24 ounce ration of bread. That's how we lived. But this was still a corrective labour camp. At least it was not *Berlag*.

* * * * *

Later we were sent to the village of Talon for agricultural work; we remained there for three years, working on the farms. But by then the *Berlag* had been organised, and we were brought there.

This camp regime was much harsher. The *Berlag* built barracks at the fourth kilometre mark in Magadan. From there we walked to work in the city. We built buildings in Magadan. Specifically, I built the prison near the store 'Chaika', both the main building and the garage. It took a long time to build.

The living and working conditions in the *Berlag* were even worse than I had suffered before. We worked on construction. We dragged stone. We rolled them up a gangway to the third floor in wheelbarrows. One woman would pull it up with a rope and another would push from below. We carried this unfinished concrete to the third floor. Doubtless you've noticed the parapet on the roof of a building? It weighs a ton, perhaps more. Two people dragged all this up there by hand. The wheelbarrows were heavy. On top of that, if on a whim the supervisor decided that the blocks of concrete were too small, then he deemed them broken and issued other, bigger ones.

Sometimes it happened that the men did not fulfil their quota. They had to produce 102 percent to receive their bread ration. But what is this ration for a man if he's spent the whole day doing such strenuous physical labour? 24 ounces is this tiny piece of bread, and even then it was often unbaked, just dough! But apart from some kind of broth, that was all they had to live on.

In the village of Balagannoe, for example, it worked like this. Someone would go to catch fish. The fish passed through our hands, all fresh. We would return to the camp, and then work the night shift. During the day other people cooked food for us from some kind of year-old fish from rusty cans. It stank! It was terrible! People got very sick from this broth. Some people ate it. I, for one, could not eat it. I would drink water and eat a small piece of bread. I divided it into three parts so that there was enough for morning, lunch, and evening. And hot water and three ounces of sugar every 10 days. That's how much we were given. But nevertheless we survived!

There was no correspondence. In the beginning it was completely forbidden. Later we were given the chance to write a letter twice a year. Well, sometimes through the 'free' mail, we could get some kind of news in or out of the camp, but this was all strictly forbidden and carried a hefty punishment if we were caught.

In 1953 Stalin died. Those who had only a short time left to serve began to be released. For good work, we were freed from the convoy guards and sent to work at *Invalidka*. Even here, there was a camp, but the regime was not as strict for them.

* * * * *

I served out my sentence to the end, to November 20th 1954. The last nine months I could go about without a convoy guard. This privilege was given to me nine months early because my work had been so good. And then I was released.

I remember my release very well. We were already working at *Invalidka* without a guard. One girl was supposed to go to the hill to gather Japanese stone pine. A light snow had fallen. It was damp. I went to check on her – I thought that if she was coming back, I would help her. She was supposed to come with a horse. She came back a little earlier than I expected, while I was still making my way up the hill.

And suddenly I hear her shout at me from a distance.

"Go back!"

What could possibly have happened?

We meet.

"Go back. You are going to the city. You are being released!"

152

We got to the guardhouse. There was a guard there, young and handsome, but somewhat shell-shocked. They had told me that he had a fearsome temper, but early in my time there, I had somehow found a way to relate to him. If he sent me somewhere to work, I never refused. He said: "Danilko, gather your things. You are going to the city now."

My clothing was all wet. You know, we were given such simple, ragged black stockings. And they were all wet. They were stuck to my legs; my legs were all black. I had been climbing the hill in wet snow.

"I am not going anywhere like this."

And he shouts: "What's that? You're not going?"

"I am going to my father, to my mother; I am going out in public. I will not go like this. I am all wet. I need to wash, to put myself in order."

"No, you will go!"

"No, I will not go like this!"

And so I went to the barrack. I went to the woman who worked in the bathhouse to get warm water to wash with and to dry everything out before the next day. She raised her voice. But I said: "Do not shout at me. I am now free." She said nothing, turned and walked off.

In the evening there was the roll call. We all lived there in the barrack, both the female convoy guards and the brigade of prisoners.

The guards come with the camp supervisors: "Where is our free one?"

They approach, but now they speak completely differently. Everything has calmed down by now.

"Well, where will you go?"

I answer: "Our girls who have already been released are there in the city. Maybe someone will take me in."

They tell me: "If there is no room, then come back, return, and we will take you in."

There are peasant huts here, like earthen dug-outs.

"The blacksmith," they say, "will do everything. We'll put a small stove in."

"I'll see."

The next morning the old man who brought the bread – he was a good person – agreed to drive me. They knew at the guardhouse that I was leaving. They asked him to wait for me. The guards approached: "Good luck with your life!" Before that, they had herded us round like cattle. But now I was free; I was determined that I would not leave wet and black with dirt. And I didn't.

* * * * *

At first we did not have passports. We were just given a certificate that was called a 'wolf's ticket'. Every month we had to report at the commandant's office. Plus I had been sentenced to two and a half years of exile. This was not at the trial, but here. The locals had announced this initiative. There was also a note in my passport about my situation and a mark which was known to them so that we could be distinguished by our passports. So we lived with this passport. And only if you were rehabilitated were you allowed to change your passport. It was 1986 before I was rehabilitated. Yes, I received my official papers, but by then I was already living on my pension!

When I was released, I was welcomed into a new job. Back then it was very difficult to find any work; but I managed to get fixed up with a job at the clinic. Of course, I could always have got work at the sewing factory, but there they expected you to fulfil a quota. After 10 years of camp life, I was fed up with quotas. I just wanted a little peace.

I was treated well at work, and I was all set to take a nursing course – yes, even back then there were such courses! But then I gave birth to my daughter. Living conditions were very difficult. There was no one to rely on for help. We earned very little.

Work was taxing – back then the working day was nine hours; Saturday was also a working day. In the beginning, I worked in different departments. Later I was transferred to the x-ray department, where I then remained. You know, your years of service add up. I went on my pension early, at the age of 45, so I was only given part of my pension. I worked in the x-ray department for more than 25 years.

Nevertheless, while there was no rehabilitation granted to me, I felt hurt. I worked for 33 years, but I do not even have the title 'veteran'. Nothing. So many times they have offered: "Here, we will give the title to you for your work." They talk; they speak at great length, explaining to me how it will be – and then nothing.

* * * * *

I had a good husband. We supported each other. At first he worked in the building trade, because he had work experience as a brigade leader even before his time in prison. Later he went to study and was transferred to work with vehicles. Then he worked in the control office as a mechanic, operations supervisor. But he met an early death; he passed away aged just 54.

I am not in good health now. High blood pressure torments me. I no longer leave my home. I have suffered a stroke. It passed, but I cannot walk. It is painful. So I only walk at home, thank God.

For me the most awful thing in camp was that we were all under guard. We walked in formation with numbers on our backs and foreheads. The guards were accompanied by dogs and carried rifles with bayonets. It was so oppressive. And how ugly we were! It was very, very depressing. What a crowd of people! And then the constant roll calls…

I remember the camp administration decided to establish a free day. But instead of giving people at least a little time to rest, they forced them to go up on one of the hills. This was where the 'Mask of Sorrow' monument for the victims of political repression is now. Below, at the 4th Kilometre, was a transit camp with men on one side and women on the other. And we did not just go up the hill, we had to bring back stone. Well, whatever stone you could take, you carried, as long as you were not empty-handed. Or we were forced to drag firewood back. It was hard. Good weather, bad weather – go, it is after all your free day.

How they beat us, humiliated us, and called us different names, especially during the interrogations! Whoever could, held out. And whoever signed various slanders, gave in because they could endure no more.

* * * * *

155

Faith, of course, helped us to stand our own ground. After all where and to whom could you turn but to the Lord? Oh, Lord, God! We prayed. And we were put in punishment cells for this. One time we celebrated Easter, but it was forbidden in camp. We all sat there and said our prayers. We also wanted to sing, but they discovered us – and put us into lock-ups, especially those who were the instigators.

We sang very little – everything was work, work. We came back to the barrack barely alive, and then lights out. When could you sing? This was the regimen. Everything was forbidden. Oh, I used to love to sing.

There is little good that I can remember. Of course, we helped each other when we were living in freedom. Our people held together. Someone found work somewhere, and fixed someone else up with a job, who had not been able to find work. We helped one another to build our homes. And we helped each other with shelter, even if we had to crowd in together.

Every possible torment befell us. That is why I never want to remember. Right away my heart aches. It was only sometime in 1960 when the judgment against me was repealed and I was able to register normally. From that moment, they began to give me the financial and civil supplements given to everyone else living in the north.

After the impact of the conditions on my health, I suffered miscarriages. I could not become pregnant. And when I was finally pregnant with my daughter, and was put on bed rest for two weeks, I was paid only 12 roubles for this time. I was paid just 12 roubles, one rouble for each day, because I was one of the 'repressed'.

We were a silent people. We were afraid, so very afraid of everything. We did not vote – after all we were "enemies of the people." We had to buy government concessions – sometimes we would spend our whole salary. And we were silent. Each month we had to report to the commandant's office. This too was like the hard labour camp. We would go and be faced with an enormous line. They spoke very rudely as if I was not a human being. "You've already started work? Why? When? How?"

* * * * *

When I was in *Berlag*, the guards always tormented us. They looked at us so evilly. They walked with their dogs and pointed their bayonets at people, their faces black with rage.

* * * * *

I remember how they brought camp inmates to the city, those who had been in detrimental conditions. This was considered the third category, that is, those who were in such an appalling state of health that they had been written off. Every one of them had scurvy; they were sick and weak. Do you think they gave them help? They herded them out to cut lumber on the hill at Snezhnaia Dolina. How many old stumps are out there – they were the ones who cut down this forest! These cripples were led out in two or three brigades. Even those who were on their deathbeds were forced out to work. And in the evening not everyone returned. They were left there up on the hill.

When the day-care centre was built on Portovaia Street, not far from me, oh, so many human bones were dug up! And where the Orthodox Church is, the Church of the Holy Spirit – how many reburials took place when that was built!! And if you go below the surface, then you find all these buildings stand on bones. That's how it is. It is from those cruel, cruel years. How many died from the cold, from sickness, from scurvy and malnutrition, from inhumane torture!

When we were brought here we were young and beautiful. My braids were magnificent!

After the war was won, so many people said to us: "We defeated Germany, but you, you are traitors to the Motherland." But we were not traitors. We were just taken from our homes!

Such was my life. That is how it passed.

157

A memorial to a victim of the camps deep in the forest.

An improvised Cross marks a mass grave where hundreds of victims of 'repression' lie at rest.

Bronislava Klimavichute (right) and her friend on the day of their release from the camps.

Bronislava Klimavichute (left).

Above: Bronislava Klimavichute (left) and friends from the camps after being released.
Below: Bronislava Klimavichute with Yletka the horse, 1954.

Above: Olga Alekseievna Gureeva in her youth before her arrest.
Below: Olga pushes her baby son, Volodia.

Above: Sofia Kononenko in happier times.
Below: Working as a cook in the day care centre after her release.

Sofia Kononenko in traditional dress.

Life outside the camps for Stepan Mudrii and friends.

Stepan Mudrii with the men's choruses that have brought him so much pleasure. During his time in the prison camps, he organised a chorus and, following the relaxation of some rules following the death of Stalin, they even performed some concerts.

Happier days from Polina Vasilevna Ens' photo album.

Above: Anna Portnova (centre) and friends in traditional dress.
Below: Anna Portnova with her husband Yuri (left) and as a young woman (right).

Solitude cells at one of the prison camps.

Solitude cells at one of the prison camps.

A guard tower from one of the local prison camps, now on display in the regional museum in Magadan.
Image from the museum display in Magadan, Russia.

Above: A painting of some of the steam ships used to transport prisoners from the Vladivostok region to the mines and camps of Magadan.
Below: A section of a camp fence with barbed wire and guard tower.
Images from the museum display in Magadan, Russia.

Maria Ivanovna Vatsyn

Born: 1928
Where: Polonka, Lutskova
area, Volynsk region
Country: Ukraine
Arrested: Autumn 1946
Sentence: 10 years labour, plus
5 years deprived of
rights
Released: December 1954
Rehabilitated: 1992

I WAS BORN IN 1928 IN THE VILLAGE OF POLONKA, in the Lutskovo area of the Volynsk region. At that time, this territory belonged to Poland, and people weren't under Soviet rule. Our entire family – Papa, Mama, my brother and I – lived there. We lived well. We considered ourselves middle class, working a small plot of land. We produced everything we needed, planting wheat, rye and barley. We had a large garden. We paid our taxes. I remember Papa carting sacks of wheat and rye. Not only were we not hungry, but we were prosperous. Our family was very hard working.
We weren't involved in politics; we took care of our own, we lived, and worked hard.

Here Ukrainians, Poles, Germans, Czechs and Jews all had friendly relations with each other, like one family. The Germans, Poles and Jews lived in the city of Lutsk, running their stores. In the summer they went to the country to their *dachas*. We children studied and played together: we went to the same schools, were friends, played and had fun as usual, paying no attention to nationality. I finished seventh grade. Most of my school years were under the Germans. Then came the Soviets.

In the autumn of 1946 they arrested me.

Papa was still out working; Mama had gone to town. My brother was working in the garden; we had finished digging up the potatoes. We heard the dog barking, and saw that some people had gathered in our yard, so I went up to them. Men in uniform were following the orders of the highest ranking officer there, who was wearing a mask. They searched the house. Since we weren't doing anything illegal, we thought that it must be some sort of mistake. The search turned up nothing whatsoever, but without any explanation, they took me to the local council.

There were already many young women there. Later they brought a vehicle and took us to the Lutsk prison. All the girls were held together. Then the man in charge came and moved us apart, far from one another. I don't know how long we were held like that. Finally we were all put in different cells and the interrogations began.

They accused me of having connections to the underground movement. I knew that this was all lies and libel, but what could I say except that I was innocent? Of course I didn't have any such connections!

During the inquest, I was not personally tortured or beaten, but several others were. Few were spared this fate while they were incarcerated; some had needles stuck under their fingernails, or were beaten on the soles of their feet. We knew that they had beaten some of the girls by the many bruises and abrasions they had. After these beatings they would be sent back to the cells where we were. Some were sobbing, others were unconscious. I remember at one of my interrogations, the interrogator laid a gun on the table. Why he did that I don't know.

The inquest into my 'case' took almost half a year. Then the tribunal sentenced me to 10 years hard labour and five years deprived of rights without appeal. When they led us out of the hall, I saw my mother. She was standing by herself, afraid to come closer. I yelled to her not to worry, I had received a 'light' sentence. The guard hit me hard with his rifle butt for that, which was painful for almost a year.

They transferred us to a camp in 1947. Here many of the guards 'poured out their souls' bullying us. Thankfully, God had mercy on me that time.

Before they sent us off, we were called in to the investigator, and I remember he asked me: "What do you choose – to eat pies, ride in a carriage, or polar bears?" I answered: "Polar bears". No one was interested in whether we were guilty of what we were accused of or not; we were all sentenced under Article 54 UK RF.

* * * * *

They sent us by stages to Taishet. We were taken in trucks that looked like they were made for transporting cattle. We travelled for a long time and slept side by side to keep warm. There was a barrel full of smelly red fish. We collected snow, so that there was something with which to slake our thirst.

In Taishet, everyone sentenced under Article 54 or 58 was placed in a large barrack with an open floor.

Here we had our fill of tyranny. Those condemned under Article 58 were considered political prisoners, and should have been held separately. But the political prisoners and the criminals were held together. If we had some sort of clothing with us, the criminals would steal it from us. For example, I had a scarf and jacket of a special cut, and they were stolen by the criminals.

The tyranny also extended to the camp officers.

The men in the camp were put to work constructing barracks and a hospital. We spent more than a year there. I remember that the regime wasn't too strict; we could even go out of the 'zone' without a guard. We went to the forest and gathered a grass, called *sarnyak*, which reminded me of the taste of garlic.

Then they took us to the bay of Vanino, and held us there for almost a year.

We set off for Magadan in 1949 – I remember that while at sea, the ship had a leaky hold and we were able to collect water to drink.

Here in Magadan, they sent me to a camp in Xinikandzh. They separated those of us condemned under Article 54 and 58 from the common criminals. Those sentenced under these articles were sent to barracks, formed into brigades, and sent to construct mines. We prepared the land for construction, clearing it of stones. Using sledge hammers and spikes, we had to 'drill' the ground for the explosives. The ground was frozen so it was very hard work.

We worked in pairs: one would hold the spike; the other would hit it with the hammer. Gradually we would make holes big enough to insert the explosive and blast away a layer of earth. In this way we 'turned over' the rocky soil. Then we had to clear the area of the rocks. After this they immediately began to build a light railway and again we had to work on all the different aspects of construction.

No matter how difficult the work was, God gave me strength and health, protecting me. Only faith and prayer helped in such a situation. I know that my mother was constantly praying for me. It was always dangerous work, I never had any safe assignments – plus we were weak from hunger.

They fed us very, very poorly. The menu was the same everyday. We received 10 and a half ounces of poor quality bread and a biscuit of flour, called 'hardtack'- just like they feed to pigs. We got an extra portion of meal as a reward for fulfilling our quota of work. We only survived all these hardships because youth was on our side.

People did die, though not often. Once, two girls were sent to clear out a heap of rubble from an excavation, to prepare it for mining ore. The upper layers gave way and buried the girls alive. It took us four days to dig out their bodies. They said that one of the girls had only two days left before she finished her sentence.

"Today it was them, tomorrow it could be me," I thought then. "Such is life."

It was difficult, but I wasn't afraid. In the course of the dull camp days, when nothing ever changed for the better, I had to come to terms with my fate, whatever it turned out to be. My emotions become dormant. Yet, every once in a while, something would happen to one of the other prisoners that unwittingly reminded me of my remaining life.

One inmate only had a few hours left before he was to be freed. We knew about this and wanted to share his joy at his long-awaited freedom after serving such a lengthy sentence. However, instead of celebrating with a former prisoner who had obtained his freedom, we were all plunged into shock as the commandant of the camp walked in bearing a tray on which was the head of this unfortunate fellow. I have no idea why they did this. Perhaps it was to create fear. But the thing I feared most in the camps was the bed bugs. I was horrified by them more than anything else.

I'm naturally easy to get along with; I readily like people, and quickly adapt to new situations. Maybe it was this quality that helped me survive all that happened after my arrest.

The one fear that I constantly felt was the fear of losing my family. Before being released, there was not even the possibility of letting my parents know where I was. They knew that I had been sentenced, but had no idea of my fate, or even whether or not I was alive. There were several attempts to send letters via civilian workers. Many of them took letters for us and mailed them as their personal mail. They helped us a lot, even though it was a big risk for them, fraught with danger if they got caught. Several of these letters reached their destination.

The turning point came in the summer of 1953.

As usual, the prisoners were led out of the camps accompanied by guards to work in the mines in Xinikandzh in Bushuy – in Vostochniy. In roll call, before being sent to work, we heard on the radio that Stalin's health was deteriorating. The Leader had a high temperature.

I didn't understand why Russian prisoners were crying. I never meddled in politics; I only knew that Stalin was The Leader. The overall mood didn't concern me.

At the end of the shift, when we came out of the mines, we saw that the flag was draped in black, the sign of mourning. We were told that Stalin died. I especially remember that day. Usually at the end of every shift, the guards led us back to the barracks where we lived. But today, our brigade leader informed us that we were to be taken back at the end of the second shift. Many thought that they were going to shoot us.

Who could have imagined then that the time had come for a long awaited change? The end of hard labour was near. Instead of being taken to the firing squad they led us to the dining hall, where large tables had been set, even covered with red cotton tablecloths. The commandant, cultured and educated, the powerful head of the camps, stood up to meet us. When we had all come in, there was complete silence. They announced that from this day forward we could send mail. We could make contact with our relatives again.

There followed several other indulgences in our lives. They decided that there would be a little commerce in the camps. We would be able to buy margarine or canned foods. When the camp commandant came into the barracks, he closely checked everything. He demanded that we keep things clean, and behaved well with those left incarcerated. He rewarded subordinates who carried out their duties well. He was pleased when he saw the well-kept, clean rooms. He was particularly pleased to see the clean white bedding of the prisoners. He talked to our brigade leader with respect, was friendly and watched out for members of the brigade.

It often happened that the bedding which we sent to the laundry came back dirty or grey. He punished them for this, demanding that they treat us as they should. He saw to it that we got new bedding when the old sheets had worn out. And to that end, they brought in white fabric which we could buy and use to make bedding.

By the way, I always loved to do hand work in my free time, which I learned as a young girl. I was always doing something, sewing or knitting. So from that time on I would decorate our bedding with embroidery, and I loved to do cross-stitch.

* * * * *

After some time an order came to release some of the prisoners. My name was on that list, and I was released at the end of December 1954. Up until then, all the money we earned had gone on to our account, and so I had a small sum.

I had served eight years, six months and 15 days. At first after my release, I was very much afraid of people and didn't trust them. I could sustain a friendship only with those who were familiar with camp life. This included several civilians.

After our release, they settled us in dormitories in the village of Xinikanzh. I worked in a factory. They gave us a certificate which temporarily allowed us to travel if we got it stamped. But they didn't give us passports, so for a long time we were unable to go anywhere.

At the end of 1955, I married a former prisoner from Kostrom, and in 1956 we set out to find somewhere to make our home. I had wanted very much to return to Ukraine. But after my arrest, my entire family had been

166

deported to Siberia. So we travelled to them in the city of Kiselev, in the Kemerovsk province. It was the first time I had seen my parents in so many years of being separated from them!

Soon they even gave us a passport. I remember what a joy it was to at last be recognised as a full citizen of the Soviet Union. I could go wherever I wanted and look for work wherever I wanted. When we had headed for Siberia, it had been our intention to stay and live there. We had taken all our things, a record player, lots of kitchen utensils, and clothes. But we didn't like Siberia. And my parents intended to return to Ukraine. So leaving all our stuff with my parents, we soon returned to the North and my parents returned to their homeland, to Polonk in Ukraine.

Of course, no one was waiting for them there. Everything that they had had before they were deported had been stolen or looted, and their home burnt. They returned to an empty place, built a little hut and tried to start life again. All they had was the shelter of this little hut to sleep in; there wasn't even a bathroom. It's not possible to live like that.

My father was ready to accept the inevitable, but mother was a fighter by nature, energetic, not fearing anyone or anything. She went to the local council, found the person in charge, and told him everything – how much was left of everything, how they had unjustly lost their house, land, farm and animals, and how, except for a box of things they had thrown together, they had nothing left.

He listened and then said: "Efimia Stepanovna, you go back and I'll come right away." Mama returned home without much hope. But he soon arrived with a tape measure and measured off 18 *sotok* of land. Though the major portion fell on land that the neighbours had already planted, he gave it to us to use. People helped us to dig and plant a garden. And despite the fact that they planted later than usual, my parents had a good harvest.

With time, my parents were able to build a home. They dug a well, built a cellar, put up a fence, acquired chickens and a young pig. We helped them to do this.

* * * * *

When we returned to Xinikanzh, my husband continued to work in the mine, and I in the factory. There are great tracts of fertile land there, lots of fish and an abundance of berries and mushrooms on the hills. After work, we would take a basket and go out on the hills, where all the bounteous fruits of nature were ours for the taking. We also had our own garden and greenhouse where we grew potatoes, greens, dill and onions, so that we always had our own vegetables. My husband would also hunt and fish.

In 1964 I gave birth to a daughter. She now works as a manager.

In 1968 we moved to Magadan. We had some savings to buy what we needed.

From the beginning we would help our friends. The people with whom we made friends with – who had shared the same fate as us – became lifelong friends, with whom we still correspond.
My best friend lives near to me, Maria Ivanovna Makovetsk. We see each other along with Antony Xaritonov Novosad, with whom we had worked. Xibirov left for his homeland. He's the one I worked with in the mine. Antony is a special friend. He's my fellow Ukrainian, who grew up in a village not far from mine.

In Magadan, I worked in the mechanical shop. I was a florist, a technical worker and linen-keeper. Once the director came in and said in front of everyone: "This isn't a garage, it's a small flower shop." I had every window and shelf full of flowers. Gorgeousness was everywhere. I remember it even now!

While still in Xinikanzh, my husband worked as head clerk. When we moved to Magadan, he found work at the power station. We received documentation about our rehabilitation in 1992. I was rehabilitated in Magadan. But they said that it was necessary to write to Lutsk for a certificate of your rehabilitation. That year they paid us a small sum of money.

At work, my boss always respected me. But many others experienced discrimination, being called bandits or fascists. They didn't want to believe that anyone could be condemned without cause.

Of course there were people who had aided the partisans. And even among them were those who were forced to cooperate against their will out of fear of being killed. However the great majority of the repressed were innocent.

When I heard accusations being thrown at me, I usually answered: "I'm not a thief; I have nothing to be ashamed of." Of course, different people react to you differently.

We have been in this apartment for 25 years already. There is another family on this landing with whom we are good friends. We try to get along together, sharing our sorrows and joys with each other. We have lots of friends in Estonia, Latvia, Kiev, Barnaul and Moscow who write and always invite us to visit.

This is how we have lived all these years. Many were the joys, dangers and sorrows. The years in the camps damaged my health. I've already had two heart attacks, and a mild oedema.

I always prayed. In the camps, I prayed to God, day and night. I once had a vision of angels appearing before me, together with the Blessed Mother. I understand that only He gave me the strength and courage to survive.

After we had loaded a truck full of ore, there were almost 10 free minutes to sit for a bit till it returned. We could take a breath and renew our strength. I prayed at this time. All the time, especially in the difficult years, God showed his mercy to me and saved me. I believe in God, and know that he exists. I talk to my daughter and grandson about faith, and teach them prayers.

My son-in-law is in the army, but he was baptised in the Orthodox Church and wears a cross.

Now I am no longer able to get to Church. It's very dangerous in my condition to go out. We called a priest and he came and blessed our apartment. I pray as I am able. Morning and evening and during the day, using my own words, I ask God for help. And now God gives me strength. I am thankful that I am able to fix my meals and take care of myself – even though my daughter and grandson also take care of me!

My children are very good. They watch over me, not allowing me to do anything myself. But really, is it easy to sit and do nothing? I can't just sit without something to do. I want everything to be washed and ironed properly. I always used to keep myself busy in our little garden, with currant and raspberry bushes. In the winter we prepared salted cabbage, and made different salads.

It seems to me that I could go on for years, yet there is still much I want to do. It's too bad that age and health hinders it. I only want to do good. My heart sings. It always wants to sing.

God has helped me not to be embittered by my deprivations and taught me to live.

Evgenia Alexandrovna Vadova

Born: April 15th 1913
Where: Korsun, Kiev province
Country: Ukraine
Arrested: October 1946
Sentence: 10 years of hard labour,
               plus 5 years deprived of
               rights
Released: 1954
Rehabilitated: 1992

I WAS BORN IN THE 300th YEAR OF THE HOUSE OF ROMANOV, at the end of their reign. One of my ancestors was rewarded by General Alexander Vacilevich Suvorov with a sword and fertile land in the Chernovitsk region. All of my relatives on my mother's side worked on the railway. No one had any other profession, from a simple telegraph operator, to the divisional manager of all transportation. Everyone worked on the south-west railway out of Kiev – that was our trade. In practically every station there was an uncle, or aunt, or cousin, or relative, so that I knew that line forward and back.

My father, Alexander Vacilevich Dmitriev, was a pure-blooded Russian, of ancient lineage and well-known nobility. Our line began even before Suvorov. This is the tale my aunt, who raised me, told me. It's too bad that when I was little and they were telling me all of this, I didn't pay too much attention. At that age your genealogy doesn't interest you. I only remember the little that I caught.

Papa finished the Kiev Cadet's corps in 1901, but didn't want to be an officer. One needed deep pockets to be an officer – you needed to be fitted out with splendid uniforms, a good horse and weapons – and Papa's family was already of the poorer nobility. So he became a French teacher. At first he taught somewhere part time, and then was invited to be tutor for my mother's father – Rafael Ivanovich. Thus he met my mother and they married. My father had a good education and was of good stock, which at that time was important. Grandpa worked as the general director of the railway, first on the 'Odessa Main' and then the 'Odessa-Oknits' line.

Gramps got Papa working: first as a cashier, then as a station guard, then station manager – not in big positions. Mama, of course didn't work; women at that time had babies. I was the seventh and next-to-last child. In the '20s little Tanya was also born, but she died. I was seventh. Everyone worked on the railway, Grandpa, Papa, all my aunts and uncles, as I've said. Grandfather was also the head of the KVZhD transportation in China. I still remember how mother with six children visited Grandpa in Xarbin, China. It was 90 years ago. They sent us in a special carriage with its own conductor.

In the '20s there was a serious typhus epidemic in Ukraine, which spread throughout the country. And in one week, we lost three people: Papa, and my two sisters, 17-year-old sister Olga and 12-year-old Maria. Yes, in one week, we saw three loved ones go to their graves. It was a terrible time.

My brother Nicholai also caught it, but lived, somehow overcoming the disease. Of all who came down with it, he was the only one who did. He died back in 1976. He had studied at the Nezhinski teaching institute, in the chemistry-technology department, and then worked as a chemist and school principal in the city of Sumax, Konotope.

Mama after all her loses, died a year after Papa.

Thus I barely remember my parents, and was left an orphan at seven years old. Three of us children were put in an orphanage in Kazatin, leaving only my older sister, Lidia, at home. Then mother's cousin, Olga Rafaelovna Baberin, took me to live with her in 1923. Aunt Olga for many years was a mother for me.

All in the family were believers, especially my uncle, who was a strong and deeply faithful person. I was a little afraid of him, unlike my aunt, who I adored. He not only knew the railways, but was also a specialist engineer-architect.

* * * * *

My family moved around a lot. At first we lived in Lipovets, then in 1926 we moved to Berdichev, to Gaivoron in 1927, and then the family moved to Kiev. After finishing seven years of school, I entered the newly established institute of finance economics. But there they forced the students to join the young communist league. My uncle, being a deep believer and not sharing communist ideals, was absolutely against that and so I had to leave the institute.

The next year I again enrolled, this time in the institute of culture, and again my uncle objected when there was talk of the communist league. My uncle had many icons in his apartment, and his religious ideology would not allow me to be a young communist.

Only in 1931, at the railway training centre, which was free and did not demand we join the young communists, did he allow me to study.

After the second year, while on training, I met my future husband, Vyaseclava Koderabek, a Czech. After the death of his father, he had moved with his mother, Bogamila Josephovna, from Vladivostok to Gaivoron. In Vladivostok, after finishing at an institute, he worked as a *stevedore*, loading ships at the sea trade port. Besides this, he was also a technical specialist surveyor. His mother had two sisters who lived in Gaivoron.

After he met me, he never returned to Vladivostok, but found work as a bookkeeper with the railway. He waited while I finished my education in Kiev.

I married Vasaslava in 1933. There was no wedding celebration; our nuptials were at the height of the famine of 1933. We barely survived such hunger. And I moved into my husband's house, with a small suitcase containing all my worldly possessions.

In 1934 our daughter, Ludmila, was born (she died three years ago); and on January 9th 1937 our son, Vyasalav, who was such a good son, was born. Such great joy, we have a son! Now he lives in Pervoyralsk, in the Cverdlovsk region. He found work in the financial sector, in the bureau of material-technical acquisition, as a bookkeeper-cum-cashier.

* * * * *

Suddenly disaster struck. On January 14th 1938 they arrested my husband. He served, at that time, as the main accountant at work, a very intelligent accountant. They had already invited him to take a position of greater responsibility in Kiev. But suddenly he was arrested. It was the end of happiness.

I immediately lost my job too, being the wife of an enemy of the people. Less than a fortnight later, I was given 24 hours to get out of our state apartment, along with my mother-in-law and two little children. We were simply thrown on to the street. My daughter was three years old, and my son, barely one year old. Mama (I always called my mother-in-law 'Mama') was old, thin, and weak, and – O woe! – her one and only son had been arrested.

We went to her sister's, to aunt Slava. She had retired from the railway and now had a one room apartment. She took us in. It was February 23rd 1938. My husband had been arrested on January 14th, just after we had celebrated the New Year (according to the old calendar). We had eaten rice with honey, cooked up a lot of *yzvar,* and simple *borscht.* After that he went in to work, and that was that – he never returned. God, how strange it was.

I couldn't find work for a long time – who would hire the wife of an enemy of the people? Wherever I went, it was always the same response: "No, no we won't take you." I went around looking half-frantic; how could I not? My well-known husband had been arrested, my children were so little and I had an elderly mother-in-law. Three people were dependant on me. Good Lord, how difficult it was.

At last, through a distant relative, I was able to get my old job back as bookkeeper-cum-cashier. At first it was only temporary, a trial period. But as there weren't many with my education, they kept me on and little by little they began to forget that I was the wife of the people's enemy. I continued to work there until the beginning of the war. I was to be sent on a course and become the head bookkeeper, but war came instead.

* * * * *

My husband also had to suffer in the camps, from which he never returned.

He first sat for three months in the Vinnitsk prison. Then they sent him to the Komi republic. From the beginning he was set to work on manual

176

labour. He would only write where he was and what kind of work he had to do. He dug, cut lumber, built railways – it was called the northern railway construction project. He was also sent to Kotlas, Syknyvkar, Ust Usolck, and other places; all the most difficult work.

But after a year and a half or two years, they needed a bookkeeper, and they made him head bookkeeper. He was a very good bookkeeper, very good. He worked in that capacity until 1945, when he started to write that he was having stomach pains.

"But don't you worry about it, its probably just indigestion, everything will be fine! I'll come home and under the care of my loving wife and mother, I'll get better.

"The main thing is to watch over the children, I'll be returning home all the same."

He was in fact able to write quite often to us. I on the other hand, in the nine years I was to spend in the camps, never had even a piece of paper. But he worked with paper, and so could send us a letter about once every two months. He wrote that soon he would be free and it would all be over.

We began to expect him in the summer of 1945. Since we had five chickens, Mama started to lay eggs aside, so that when Slava came, he wouldn't have to eat punishment rations. He wrote that he wasn't feeling very well, but then it seems he relaxed and was already better, and so I felt better too.

My husband wrote that he had a good friend who worked as a veterinarian. But we felt through his letters, that something wasn't quite right. Another letter came, from Moscow this time, explaining that he was pleading his case, seeking a just decision, but still hadn't received a positive answer.

In the beginning of October, I come home from work to find my poor little mother-in-law crying:

"Come woman, read this letter from the camp."

"Dear Evgenia Alexandrovna," it begins, "We all, the friends of your husband, want to express our condolences…."

Vyaseslav died, after an operation on his liver, of cancer. Officially everything was covered up. His friend the veterinarian wrote to tell us the news. He wrote that they had buried him as a free man, erected a monument and said their farewells.

Mama was so upset, wondering if they had said prayers over the grave, hoping that perhaps they had found a priest – after all they had not been spared the camps either. They had buried Vyaseslav outside of Kotlas, a railway town.

It was all for nothing; they had gained nothing. He wasn't yet 29 years old when they arrested him, and he died at age 37. They ruined as good a man as he for no reason, and gained nothing.

And on October 28th, they arrested me.

* * * * *

But even before my arrest, we had to survive the war alone. On the morning of June 22nd, my boss, who lived above us, came running and yelling: "The war has started!"

I didn't believe it at first, the day was so clear and wonderful. We took bleach and started to do the laundry. Then on the street, over a loudspeaker, we heard Stalin: "Today at four in the morning, our enemy traitorously attacked our country… We will not give up even an inch of land."

But Stalin abandoned Ukraine to her fate. At the start of the war, we heard Stalin; at the end, Hitler over Berlin.

The war began. I had just begun to get on my feet a little bit, to get a little pay, and a little bit used to it, and then I began to weaken. It was very difficult with two little children. They proclaimed war on the 22nd, but it was impossible to leave one's home as the railways were immediately turned into a war zone – they were strategic targets.

The front came closer, battles raged; I just worked. It was impossible to leave. I had no means of doing so anyway, only receiving peanuts from the railway. I was thrown out of my apartment and lived in my aunt's one room apartment.

In passing, she made this promise: "Wherever they take you, I'll not move, and I'll not let them take the children."

Battles were being waged over Kiev, and then the fighting came to Vinnits. The planes could destroy an entire train in one pass. It was terrible with children and an elderly mother. Where could we go?

Many men sent their families to Siberia, evacuating the women and children. But I was working. So I stayed where I was earning something. I often think that it was the prayers of my mother-in-law and her sister, my aunt Slava, that saved me and the children. They prayed two to three hours every day before their icons.

Then the last train was bombed and the Germans were on us, with their automatic weapons.

* * * * *

Despite the fact that my grandfather was a German, I was so frightened seeing them. I had even studied German as a child, though we never spoke it at home. To us, in our fear, the Germans seemed something terrible, strange and unbelievable. I remember hiding in the cellar of a shed. We had them in Ukraine, for storing barrels of cabbage and potatoes. We hid together with our neighbour, an engineer, and his family in his cellar. We sat and sat, then at dawn it was decided that I should go out to take a look.

I go out.

Just then a German comes around the corner, with his automatic on his hip and his grenades swinging from his belt.

I'm so frightened that I get sick and freeze.

He comes closer, yelling.

"Stand still!"

He comes up to me and pushes me down to the ground by my shoulders.

My mind is racing, full of fear and the stories of cruelty we have heard. When the Germans had taken Vinnits, there were several people hiding in a cellar, who had fired back at them. The Germans simply tossed a grenade into the cellar.

He shoves me down.

I feel like a dog in a kennel.

I freeze. I sit and can't do anything.

He doesn't do anything to me, but I can't stand from the fear.

And – oh God! – my family is in that cellar – my mother-in-law, aunt and children, my neighbour Maria Nikolaevna and her daughter!

I yell: "Kinder, Mutter! Kinder, Mutter!"

He does nothing, just looks so strange; then turns and leaves.

The war is definitely upon us.

* * * * *

There was nothing that could be done; we had to survive; that was all. The first two weeks it was difficult to find work, and I had three to feed. And then such plundering began all around. War is such a terrible thing in all its aspects, when every kind of injustice reigns freely. They pillaged the stores, the warehouses, the dairy, wherever they could. It was chaos.

Thus it was so very difficult to find work at first, but still one had to work, I had children and a mother to feed. Then an acquaintance was, little by little, able to get me work as a cashier in the dairy. I worked amongst Germans for two years at the dairy. One worked wherever one could earn a few pennies. They paid salaries just like all the others in power.

Many have described the war, writing that the Germans would indiscriminately shoot people and children on the streets. It wasn't like that with us. They didn't touch anyone, not the children, not the elderly, no one. We lived under the Germans, as under any other power.

I always worked hard, tried always and everywhere to be conscientious, and people related respectfully to me. We weren't a concern to the Germans. They kept to themselves, and we went on working. There were no problems.

* * * * *

In 1943 the Russian army was advancing rapidly towards us. Once more we awaited the arrival of the front. Of course, we began to be a little afraid. They announced that our dairy would be closed. The Russians were getting closer and the Germans had to flee. They would ship us along with our equipment to Sheptovk, near Rovno, to the next plant. And from Rovno, Zdolbunovo, the former border, is only five and a half miles. And between them is Kvasilov, where the Czech infantry columns were; my husband's people.

My mother and aunt always cried not to be taken there. They told me: "They rape the women and take the children. If you let them know that uncle Sasha is coming, they'll take the children. Couldn't you perhaps, work in Zdolbunovo, and the children stay with us in Kvasilov?"

And so they load us all on to trains at night, and send us off.

We are sent off to Kiev at night.

I see my old street, Kudryavsk, but they don't let me off.

They chase the train here and there, but are able to pull off some sort of manoeuvre in Darnits.

We all thought they would let us off in Kiev all the same, but no. The next night we heard a different language, a strange station and Polish nationalists – the pointsmen in nationalist uniforms running around with lanterns. And we naively continued asking when we would arrive at the Proskurovsk plant. What Proskurovsk? We were already in Poland! And there, due to a nervous liver, my legs grew numb; I was paralysed.

We were already in Peremyshl, and not too far from Lodz in Poland. Zdunck Vola is there, Shvinets in German, and it was there that they assigned us to various domestic jobs. I didn't walk for two months, my legs completely refused. Overall, I looked healthy, but I couldn't walk. If I stood, I would fall like a hen. My legs didn't hurt, they were just swollen, and I was so white, like linen.

But my children helped. They went around the fields digging potatoes. We spent a year in Poland. The Polish are good people. There are good people everywhere, and we made friends with several of them. But the war front began to creep close again.

The Germans gathered us Russians up again, coming to the village where we lived in a half dilapidated hut, and in 24 hours had us on a train to Germany. We were there in just two hours time. They were to take us to Munich, to some sort of plant. As we got to within 20 miles of Berlin, to the Shenevaide station, American and English planes were flying over. Berlin was burning like an out-of-control bonfire.

We should have been taken to Munich, but Berlin was burning. The Russians had already forced their way across the Oder, and were drawing near Berlin. We saw a wild ocean of fire. What a battle it was over Berlin, simply terrible! Thousands of American and English planes were flying over Berlin together. It was something terrible.

We were put on an electric train, and sent back. We were taken to some sort of German camp. There were three camps for workers from the east, from Russia, Ukraine, and Poland. And across the road – a camp for Jews. But we didn't know one another, as we were separated by two fences and barbed wire. We spent about a month and a half in this camp.

* * * * *

And at last our soldiers finally arrived.

They somehow fed the Germans, but not us, with swedes or something. My legs were still swollen like great pillars. I felt that I would never walk normally again, and I had the children to look after.

After the bombardment subsided, we were sent out to check the damage to the railway. Any strong young men were taken to repair the damage to the railway bed and to where bridges were damaged.

Then they blew up the city of Marienburg, or Marienbad – everything was burned to the ground.

At that time we sat in the woods, in trenches. The earth shook from the explosions, everything for several kilometres around. Our men who returned from the city said that all that was left was dirt, bricks, bones and blood. An entire city destroyed. We sat and prayed, whoever could, of whatever faith, in whatever language.

It was terrible in the forest. Everyone prayed. It lasted all night. In the morning the battle was drawing nearer; we hid in the basement of a six-storey building – in a bomb shelter deep underground in fact. How the Germans had equipped those bomb shelters! We hid there for half a day.

Suddenly a soldier runs up, not very tall, under 50 years old.

He's one of us, a Ukrainian, with the name of Boiko.

He is searching for his daughter, Marica. The Germans exiled her to Germany when she was 16 years old.

He has been running around everywhere, to cellars, asking if anyone has seen her.

He says someone told him that she had been with us in the camp.

He didn't find his daughter, but he helped us a lot. He told us that we had to get out of there fast, as it was impossible to bring any reinforcements in through the channel and a large battle was about to break out. He said that if we weren't able to make the crossing in an hour, they would place a rocket launcher there and shoot anyone on this bridge way. And so he led us through the ruins, through barbed wire, through the rubble of this completely ruined city.

Something strange happened. We were going in single file behind him along a trail, running. There weren't any houses there, but sometimes a corner of a house stood on its own, or a flaming pit, sometimes there was an explosion right in front of us, an obstruction, rings of barbed wire; and behind the barbed wire hung those executed.

It was terrible indeed. They let off a volley of shots; a column of land exploded, higher than the trees, higher than the buildings. We dashed from one side to another; people were falling, bullets whistling, loud explosions, rockets firing, and fear, fear. We ran for five miles, and he was with us, he was very good. He left us between some small mounds; it was quiet between them, the front line zone ran through there.

Then we saw the barracks. There were rumours that they had just led out the English prisoners of war. They took them on farther, but chased us here, and so we spent the night in those buildings. And then we went by foot through Poland always keeping in the shelter of the sides of houses. We went for two weeks, sleeping in half destroyed buildings or huts, wherever we happened to be.

We slept and then continued on. We found unharvested gardens growing where we needed them, growing potatoes and everything else. The Germans had good gardens, and so we gathered peas or squash – whatever we could find.

About seven or so miles on there was a checkpoint. Our solders were already there. Majors and lieutenants filled out information cards on us – who were we, why were we there, for what, from where and so on. How did the Germans catch you, where, what place where you in? There we went through this questioning process, filled out all the documents, registered, and they left us there for a time.

They received us well there – that is our Russians did. There were 1,020 of us there, probably more in the city of Shvibts, but it was a completely destroyed city. People of every nationality were gathered there. There were only 10 kitchens there in different regions of the city – field messes. They were large messes and they gave us soup and bread. The soup was mostly potatoes.

* * * * *

We waited there to be sent back to our homeland. But no one could leave right away, everything was occupied, busy, the trains and all the transport. And so they sent cars. They freed the troops, and began to take us by truck, in groups of 22 to 23 people, across all of Poland. We travelled though mine fields, and every kind of thing happened.

In one place the bridge had been practically destroyed, yet many vehicles were going across one after the other on makeshift wooden planks. Our vehicle made it across, but another didn't; the bridge couldn't hold, and it fell through the deck and 23 lives were lost instantly. Thanks be to God, we made it.

Then we travelled by Polish roads. To Krakow, to Ravi Russkoy but still so far from Lviv. In Ravi Russkoy they held us until the autumn. There I still had to work in the fields; I walked cutting wheat and rye.

Exactly a month after leaving Ravi Russkoy, we ended up in Siberia, in Taishet. Arriving in Siberia, we were practically naked; we were not dressed for that kind of cold at all.

We worked on timber, cutting and hauling large logs. We worked with dull saws and blunt axes on trees three arm's span in circumference. And we worked with skidders; pushing wheelbarrows along slippery paths, while we were practically faint with hunger.

And why did they treat us like that, not even giving us decent clothing? We were in such a terrible condition, it's even worse to try to imagine it. There are no words to describe it. Nakedness was the usual condition of the people there. The barracks were cold, it was raining – we laid hungry and cold, huddling with each other, trying to cover up with some sort of sackcloth. In the woods, we stepped in water with our bare feet; it was terrible.

And all around us were dogs and automatic weapons: that too was something terrible. One needed great strength to endure all of that. It's even difficult to speak about it, about what it took to survive.

There were always dogs on chains, and machine guns, three rows of barbed wire, and towers, towers. Terrible.

In the morning: "Line up in rows of five. Fall in under the waiting guards, begin marching with the right foot, if you start with the left, it will be considered an escape attempt, and you can be shot without warning." This 'chant' has been with me all my life. We knew it by heart. They almost killed me once. I had fainted, gotten my foot snagged on a root going through the woods, and gotten sick.

This was near Taishet. Two of the other girls, one on either side of me, caught me. Luckily it seems as if the guard liked one of these girls, or he would have shot me, but he had pity and didn't shoot.

When we arrived, we were already in the last stages of dysentery, and about to be overcome by disease. When I was young, around the age when I entered technical school, I was a little fat overall, 155 or 160 pounds. But in Siberia, in the camps, I weighed half that fully dressed – 88 pounds.

They fed us on jars of water, that's all. If there were a couple of grains of barley in it, that was good. We got so thin that we would fall and die on the road.

And then, much later on, they brought us uniforms from the hospital, after the war. Two or three very large trucks arrived. Padded jackets, quilted pants, sailor's jackets – all left over from the war, all covered with dried blood where their previous owner had been wounded. We were repulsed to be outfitted in clothing like that, but it was cold, and we needed something to wear.

We chose as best we could. There were no scissors (we didn't see a real pair of scissors for nine years) but still we tried to cut out the bloody places with a piece of sharpened metal, and sew in pieces without blood, as best we could. We never saw a needle either; we attached them with whatever we could. It was practically impossible to keep a needle, to hide it from the guards. So we made our own from wood. Oh, I can't tell everything – it is too, too painful.

* * * * *

When we arrived at the bay of Vanino, that is at the Pacific Ocean, I figured that the ocean had saved us. It was the spring of 1948 and they had gathered prisoners from every part of Siberia for the Camps in the north. They brought the political prisoners condemned under Article 58. Three different groups were brought there, from Lviv, from Riga, and us Russians – almost 1,000 people were gathered there in those barracks on the ocean. It was already warm. They had just taken away the Japanese prisoners, so we were replacements. They had also just taken the German prisoners of war for return to Germany from the Siberian camps. We were always passing them on the road; sometimes they would shout at us.

At the bay of Vanino we were put in large and small barracks in a camp recently vacated by the Japanese prisoners of war. We were considered only transitional, and so they didn't feed us like they did in the camps in Siberia for our work. We all received exactly the same, 28 ounces of bread; it was quite adequate, and three times a day we ate. In the morning we received thin soup and our ration of bread, or tea and bread. Distribution began at six o'clock in the morning. One brigade went at a time – they received their ration and went to the mess hall. The mess hall could hold 300 people, but there were 3,000 of us. So while one shift ate, the others waited. When one finished the next went in. It took from 6am until noon everyday for everyone to get their breakfast.

Then lunch was the same from noon to 6pm, but we didn't receive any bread at lunchtime, only in the morning. Supper was from 6pm until midnight. We were well fed there.

We who arrived from Siberia were already thin and emaciated when we reached that camp. Those who came from Lviv or the far east had only been exiled within that year and so weren't as emaciated as us. I remember when we came through Lviv; the young women were such pretty, well-fed Ukrainians.

When they arrived at the camp, they were not yet so worn out and emaciated. The Lvivians had looked after their own, allowing them to bring sacks of food from home, which had been sent on to them. They had crackers and even pieces of bacon to eat, they ate well enough that they were still recognisable as human beings.

It was the same with those from the east, who had been just been with their families. They too carried supplies from home with them, up to half the sack was filled with food – most of it dried food. Whatever they could they brought with them, so of course they were not yet completely worn away. But eventually these women disappeared; they grew thin like the rest of us.

We were already like starving dogs, mere skeletons. These other poor girls didn't even want to get up at six o'clock in the morning for breakfast. We of course, ate every crumb, but they either didn't go, or only ate half, only a little, wasting food. We were always in line waiting, and licked the last morsels off our plates where possible. If, for example, they served mush with perch – ocean perch, imagine! – we would just hope that even a little piece of perch would come our way. Even the tail, or the head – if only a little bit of something would come our way!

And when everyone has eaten, the cook still has a huge cauldron, so huge you could swim in it, which still has food in it.

And they shout: "Who wants seconds?"

We do of course and, with our bowls licked clean, we go for seconds.

So till midnight we lick up everything indiscriminately.

After the hunger which we have had to endure, we'll eat anything.

* * * * *

We waited for a steamer for a month and a half. Then we set sail, to wherever. We had received full portions of bread, had perch, and received seconds.

Well, the next stage was what they called the medical examination commission. A special Kolyma guard unit took us. On the shore in Vanino, they built barracks with large halls. There we were forced to completely undress and made to go in naked before the commission. At the end of the hall was a row of tables, and the commission – 15 to 20 men – sat behind them. They were all considered to be men of rank, but a warrant officer was considered high rank along with lieutenants, old men and other such people. We had to go in naked to where the men sat. Before beginning, they first checked all the marks on my body, writing everything down in detail; they recorded where there was a birthmark, even how many fingers I had.

Then they took a full-face photograph, and then a portrait shot. The commission checked everything. We had to sit before them three times, three times face forward, and three times with our backs to them. It was so humiliating. This humiliation has remained in my memory all my life: to stand before two dozen men in this state. And we had young girls of 17 and 18 years of age, who had to appear naked before those 60-year-old men.

And why? Basically, so that they could check that we were taking absolutely nothing with us, not a scrap of paper, not a pencil, nothing. For that we have carried this lifelong disgrace, yes, for our entire life. Of everything that has happened in my life, nothing seemed more perverse than this exhibition conveyor belt. Terrible! It was just terrible what we had to endure.

They took us to the steamship *Nogin* on November 1st and we arrived at the port of Nagayevo in Magadan on the evening of the 6th – the 31st anniversary of the October communist revolution. They didn't let us off the boat on the 7th or 8th. The boat remained at anchor right out in the centre of the bay. In 2005 I was laying in the gerontology ward of the hospital here, and I could see from my window exactly where that ship had stood, and where they unloaded us.

They began to unload us on the morning of the 9th. We climbed down the ship's ladder to a launch, which brought us to shore. I remember how the bay looked then; it still wasn't built up as it is now. But, like swallow nests, there were shacks everywhere, stuck together from driftwood and boxes. I look now, and revel in Magadan, such a handsome place. Then there were just huts, huts everywhere, all around us, made of whatever they could find, their floors made from swept dirt. That was how we saw Magadan for the first time.

When we got to shore, we immediately fell to the ground. They got us up, and we went two and a half miles to Marchikan. There weren't any roads, just a path leading away from the port – we walked through ditches and stumbled over stumps on our way to the baths.

There were long continuous barracks holding 450 to 500 people in each, with double and triple planks for sleeping side by side. We would lie back to back, like sardines in a can; it was very difficult to turn over. The sick, the healthy, the young, the old – all were put there. We lived there until the spring, doing practically nothing. I remember once they took us to gather potatoes. That was a holiday. Rarely would they even allow us to walk the 'zone'. We lived like that from November to March.

* * * * *

That spring they began to send us off to work. I was first sent to the 13 kilometre camp for two months. I didn't wear a number. You could say that I didn't wear a number at all in Kolyma. After a month or two, they called me in for an evening check with all my things, along with two other girls. We were terribly afraid, my friend and I. Many had sentences of 25 years; I had 10. They took us to the head, a lieutenant, 30 years old. He received us, but he didn't want to answer any of our questions, said it was none of our concern. But then he took pity on us and explained that my friends needed to go to another camp and await the ITL – that is a general correctional camp. We worked in that camp, just like all the other prisoners, only we didn't wear numbers. That was in the spring of 1949.

After this they took us by AH-24 airplanes to Susaman and from there by vehicle to Arkagal, a gold mine named 'the 25th of October'. I worked in a mine underground up to depths of 65 feet hauling wheelbarrows of ore. I also worked on an open firing range. I spent about two months there. Suddenly a change came; orders came to take the women from the hard labour. They sent us to work on 'light duty' and took us from working underground.

They sent us to work supplying lumber: cutting and hauling logs. From there, from Arkagal, they sent us by foot deep into the *taiga*, to Sardyna, in the Susaman area. Now it's hard to believe that there was such wilderness in the Kolyma then. I was there in Chingichinax, Xattynax, Urga-Talon – all frightful forests. That was something – to live through all that.

What saved me? First of all, I worried terribly about my children, and that kept me going. I had only one thought, to survive to see my children again. I needed my strength of will for that. And then too in the camps I had this 'romantic' thought. Every camp had its storytellers, their 'novelists': much like Evgenia Ginsburg, the famous writer. Those who could tell stories were much respected.

When we returned to our barrack from working all day, it was already dark; there was no light; somehow we would lie down – what else could we do? There were no books, no movies, no theatres, nothing to read, no way to write, nothing. What did we do among ourselves? There were only the walls and floor, not even a needle. So whoever could tell stories was highly valued. An education was valued.

I not only had a higher education, but I had read a lot, and had an excellent memory. I could tell stories from history, and from geography. I could tell them so everyone could understand. Lots of people tried, but not all were successful. I had a reputation as a good storyteller. Even if I was transferred to another camp, they would immediately know I was there and I would tell stories. They said: "Ah, Aunt Zhenya has come, she can tell stories." Thus my reputation spread, and that also helped me.

* * * * *

Of course my faith helped me a lot – it goes without saying. I have a truly authentic Christian faith. I'm Orthodox. I pray to God, of course, but mostly in my heart. It was such a hell all around us and so pagan. All day long I heard such foul language that it wasn't even possible to make the sign of the Cross. But of course in my heart I prayed.

Now I pray aloud every day. I can recite a few prayers, but every day, every day I make the sign of the Cross, and with all my heart, give God thanks.

How I survived what I did, God only knows. I experienced such horrors: aeroplanes crashing, bombs exploding nearby; and yet something saved me. May God save us from having to ever live through war again, and may God save people from ever knowing such woe again. I had thought about writing down what happened to me, but there in the camps there was no paper, not even a pencil. We could only tell each other our stories.

At best in the camps, I could buy a scrap of paper for a ration of bread, and write, though with difficulty, that I was still alive. Or once every couple of months I might receive a letter – that was all the communication there was.

* * * * *

They arrested me in October of 1946, and I served eight and a half years, being released only after the death of Stalin. They released us right there in Susuman. I'll never forget that day. They released me before my complete term was served, as I had been sentenced 10 years. From 1950 I had received marks for good work, and they counted that, and released me a year and a half early. I was judged by a military tribunal, and that was what they wrote.

With release, all my thoughts turned to my children. When I was arrested, the children remained with their grandmother, my mother-in-law. But Grandma didn't even receive a pension. But her sister, Aunt Slava, may she rest in peace, was a wonderful woman, and my husband's sister, Katya, also loved my children very much. I practically never received news from them, but no news was good news. Once, they wrote to tell me that Slavik was in the Urals with Grandmother, and Lilia with Aunt Katya.

I also remember that when they arrested me, I was planning on going to the movies, and was dressed in practically nothing; we had lived so simply. But I had such hair! It was rare to have such hair as I had, everyone admired it. I plaited my hair, braiding it like a crown. Once when Slavik was nine years old, I washed up, dressed and did my hair. There was a mirror on the bathroom table, and I saw how my son lying there, never taking his eyes off of me.

"Why are you looking at me like that, Slavka?"

His grey eyes got so big, not expecting me to have noticed him, and he ran up to me and hugged me saying: "Mama, I think you are just the most beautiful woman in the world!"

That was the day before they arrested me.

* * * * *

While I was in prison the children had grown up. Slavik was up to my shoulders, and Lilia was tall, she was already almost 12. I hadn't seen them for almost nine years. Now I was free, where would I go first? And how and with what? I still had five years without rights, and not a penny to my name. I had no means to leave. My mother-in-law had died of stomach cancer while I was still in prison.

I pray almost every day for my mother-in-law; such an extraordinary woman she was. I'll always remember how kind she was and how she did so much for me and my children. You can say that she saved us. She herself was small, unprepossessing, no education as such, but she was such a wonderful homemaker and a remarkable person with a big heart. She loved the children more than her own life; she was that kind of grandmother. She helped me in everything. Imagine being left with two little children, three years and one year old!

They stole what should have been the most happy and wonderful days and years of our lives from us. I wasn't even 25 years old when they arrested my husband, and the tribulations began. I had to work, and would not have survived without her, whatever I had done. I always knew that when I was at work, the children were at home, well cared for. She cooked, washed, sewed and knitted. She did so much good for me; it's rare to find so capable a mother-in-law. When I married her son, she took me in as her own daughter, and I called her Mama. The neighbours thought that she was my mother, not my husband's, we were so close. She was a wonderful woman. She saved my children after my arrest, along with her sister. I'm so grateful to them.

My mother-in-law had to move with her grandson to Pervouralsk, near Sverdlovsk, to a cousin of her husband's. He had invited her to come and took responsibility for her, but wanted her to take care of his children. But she brought Slavik with her, and it was obvious that they didn't like that. And for her, Slavik was her happiness. She had lost one son, and only one

The tattered clothes worn by the prisoners during their time in the camps.
Often the only clothing that was issued was that of the dead.
Images from the museum display in Magadan, Russia.

Above: Eating and cooking utensils from the camps.
Below: Wheelbarrow, communist star and a piece of mining railing used in the difficult mining of uranium ore and gold.
Images from the museum display in Magadan, Russia.

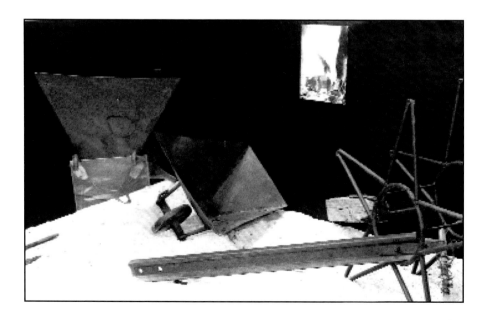

Above: Barbed wire from the camps and a sign that reads: "Forbidden zone – entrance prohibited. Will shoot."
Below: Prison bars and a wooden sled used to carry bodies of prisoners.
Images from the museum display in Magadan, Russia.

Butugichag mountains are still littered with the remains of the mining works, including convicts' boots, **above**, and old rails, pylons, barbed wire and wagons, **below** (at Sopka camp).

Above: A larch cross in a cemetery in Butugichag mountains.
Below: Remains of Sopka camp, one of the toughest camps. Located at the top of the hill, prisoners were lashed by the winter's icy winds as they worked the tin and uranium mines.

Above: The entrance to a former tin mine at Butugichag mountain camp, frozen in both winter and summer.
Below: Summer night in Magadan.

The Bay of Nagayevo, **above**, where thousands of deported convicts arrived at Magadan from the transit camp of Vladivistok. From here they were taken to the camps of Kolyma Gulag. Sofia Ivanovna Kononenko, **below**, arrived here in 1949, sentenced to 10 years of penal servitude.

Olga Alekseievna Gureeva, who was released in March 1956 after serving more than 10 years of a 25 year sentence, at the 'Mask of Sorrows' memorial, **above**, and, **below**, in the Magadan museum commemorating the Kolyma gulag.

Above: Evgenia Antonovna Voloshin shows a picture of her father, Anton Vasilovich Voloshin, who was executed by firing squad on December 8th 1937 at the age of 39.
Below: Bronislava Bronislavovna Klimavichute, who served six years of an eight year sentence.

Bronislava Bronislavovna Klimavichute shows a Rosary made out of bread in the camps. It is now over 50 years old and is on display in the chapel of the Martyrs in the Parish of the Nativity of Jesus, Magadan.

Above: Anna Korneevna Portnova and her husband, Yuri Aleksandrovich Portnov, who were married shortly after they were both released in 1956.
Below: Stepan Prokopovich Mudrii, who served eight years of a 25 year sentence. He was released in 1958. He stands on the bay of Nagayevo with his granddaughter, Oxana.

Opposite page, top and middle: Two prayer books hand-made by Bronislava during her time in the camps. The left hand one was written on birch bark at the port of Vanino in 1950.

Bottom: Sofia Kononenko embroidered these images of the Mother of God and Christ Child (left) and the Mother of God (right) in prison, using thread from shirts, dresses and pillowcases and a fish-bone needle.

This page: Letters written on cigarette papers between Bronislava Bronislavovna Klimavichute and her parents while she was in the prison camps.

Icon of the Martyrs of Kolyma in the Chapel of Martyrs, Church of the
Nativity, Magadan.

Above: The town of Magadan lies on the northern Okhost sea, in the extreme east of Siberia. Under Stalin, it was the main point of entry for hundreds of thousands of convicts sent to the Kolyma Gulag.

Below: Parishioners, including survivors of the Kolyma Gulag, with Fr Michael Shields at the Church of the Nativity of Christ, Magadan.

Above: Bronislava Klimavichute's prisoner number given to her by the NKVD, garlanded with barbed wire from the Butugichag uranium mine. The items are displayed in the Martyrs Chapel, Church of the Nativity, Magadan.
Below: The 'Mask of Sorrows' memorial overlooking Magadan.

grandson remained. She found work for some years in a nursery for the railway as a seamstress. She sewed nappies. They gave her a tiny little room. She also worked as a night watchman. She was poor, but somehow she survived.

And her sister, Aunt Slava, helped. She raised my daughter Katya. She was a doctor, as was her husband, and so, of course, they lived well. She did a lot for my daughter, whom they raised and educated.

After I was freed, they wrote to me from Pervouralsk: "Zhenya, don't be in a hurry to leave, but delay a bit, because here they will look on you askew, with suspicion."

My son, Slavik, after his Grandma died, went to work at 16 years of age, as a welder's assistant and lathe operator. And what could I do? I couldn't return in only a tattered padded jacket. How could I help my children, especially if they said: "Our mother is a prisoner"? How would they look on us then? Slavik had even enrolled in the young communists' league, and I would ruin his life if I returned. So I stayed put. And during those years of exile, my daughter married in Pavlov; and I didn't want to disturb their life either. I understood that I was a handicap; my children had already managed to grow up without me.

What could I do? I had to put my life together while I was here. I met a man, another victim of the repression, who had served 10 years in Seimchan. He was a very good man, Romanian by birth. He had been a fine Parisian tailor at one time. We fell in love with each other, but couldn't register as husband and wife; I still had five years deprived of rights, and didn't even have the right to marry.

When Stalin died, all the foreigners began to disperse back to their own countries. Then they reached an agreement to send everyone back to their homelands, and began to strictly organise everyone sending them off in plane after plane. Since I was already practically freed, we thought they would allow us to get married. But within 24 hours they had shipped him out, and, of course, what kind of communication could we, particularly former prisoners, have with foreigners?

That's how it was there, and we never saw each other again. Every aspect of life was ruined.

Eventually I married Badov. He was also a former prisoner. I put up with him for five years. At first all was fine, he was afraid to lash out in my presence. Then he began to use foul language, and play around and do no good. I was in the camps nine years living completely surrounded by foul language, never seeing anything good, but thanks be to God, not allowing myself to be caught in the same. After this marriage, I didn't even want to have another suitor, though there were few women.

But being unlucky with Badov, I didn't want any more.

I worked all my life long, in the camps and then when I was released. I worked with a cattle-herd, the best in the region. They say that there is an entire corner dedicated to me in the communal farm museum. All the magazines wrote about me as the finest hay gatherer and calf tender. That's what I knew my entire life – to work honestly and conscientiously.

I was reunited with my children only after 18 years separation. I spent nine years in the camps, and then there was no money for me to travel home, not a penny to my name. I thought I would only ruin their lives and reputation if I appeared. Nor would they give the 'former repressed' work for long anywhere. Only now have they begun to recognise us, though not with open arms; just a little mention on the Days of Remembrance. I was no good to anyone then. My mother-in-law had died, my aunt was in Kiev; I had nowhere to go.

It was 1964 before I was able to take a holiday. I travelled with my daughters from my second marriage, one 10 years old, the other eight. I have four children – Ludmilla, born in 1934, and Vyasislav, born in 1937 from my first husband, and Galina, born in 1954, and Tamara born in 1956 from my second marriage. So we went together on my first vacation. My son had written that we should come at the beginning of summer. But my boss, Nickolai Fedorovich, advised me to go later when they would have had a little of the crop from their gardens. So I listened to him.

My son and daughter-in-law had waited for my arrival in early summer, but then they went to her relatives in the country. They still had a week and a half of vacation left – and here's the kind of intuition a person can feel – but Slavka said: "Nina, we're going home tomorrow." They returned and I was already there, with my other children running in the street, and my suitcases stood in the hallway. I was with my daughter – she was setting the table and I sat and read a letter.

Suddenly someone from behind a curtain takes my hand.

My son!

At last we are once again under the same roof.

He hugs me from behind, crying: "Mamachka, my dear mother, my dear mother."

What could I do? They had arrested me; I had left two children behind…

And here he is all big and grown up, a head and a half taller than I.

We are both trembling.

He doesn't want to let go of me.

We haven't seen each other in 18 years.

Our reunion is joyful and difficult at the same time.

I cannot tell him everything that I have had to endure in this life.

* * * * *

Today I have been rehabilitated; completely exonerated, not guilty of any thing. How can people comprehend that now? And what about this life of mine, already past? I survived a war, along with all its horrors and deprivations and all that I – and only I – experienced. I could write 10 volumes. And all the same I'll say again that the very worst was the way they degraded us. I've lived through hunger, went around in tattered rags, had my hair freeze to the walls in the barracks, but its the humiliation of appearing naked before that crowd of officers that I will never forget.

Now, as a former victim of repression, they've given me a three room apartment, and put in a phone without charge. I receive money from the Solzhenitsyn fund for unjustly suffering. Money from the Solzhenitsyn fund – is that so important? Yet one kind word is priceless. Fanna Nikolaevna, the administrator of the fund, has sent me congratulations personally. Now that's priceless.

I love Solzhenitsyn very much, and Fr. Michael too. They are both very precious people to me. The meetings with the repressed that Fr. Michael hosts are holy events. I bend my knee before him with all my heart. It's all about family, about the human family. And the most precious thing is praise, so that people remain people. If we act like wolves, who will benefit from that? But if only 10 percent of the people are as good – oh, how we would live!

Eve Romanovna Anishin

Born: May 17th 1928
Where: Tuchi, Rovenski Region
Country: Ukraine
Arrested: 1950
Sentence: 25 years hard labour and 5 years deprived of rights
Released: 1956
Rehabilitated: November 20th 1997

IN 1939 WE LIVED IN POLAND. We were peasants but we worked our own land.

And in 1939 the war began; soon the Russians came.

They began to forcibly establish collective farms. At first, people did not want to go as they knew what awaited them. Several families paid for that, and many were exiled.

My mother died very young, I was only seven years old. I had a three-year-old sister. By 1940 many people already knew that war was coming, and many fled to Russia. But Papa had always been a faithful believer, and wouldn't flee. The Germans shot Papa in our own home.

Only the elderly were left in the village. None of them were guilty of anything, and yet they killed them all. The Germans rode around the village on horseback with torches, burning homes. They burnt down all the homes, and everything people had.

During the war our local school was bombed, along with everything else. I only managed to finish the fourth grade. When the Russians came after the war, five years had passed since I had been in school. Other children my age had finished the 10th grade, but I had to go back to the fifth.

Unfortunately, I wasn't able to study any more anyway, as I had to go to work. Work was all one could do; there wasn't any sort of education.

* * * * *

After the war, some people became bandits (dissenters) – those who hid in the woods, and wouldn't cooperate with the Russians.

We lived in the country. All kinds of people would come to us, saying: "Give us something to eat." We dared not refuse soldiers from the Ukrainian National Front; they were armed and had no qualms about shooting you. We tried to feed everyone who asked. People in the country were the most repressed, and yet everyone came to them, especially for food.

* * * * *

I was arrested in 1950.

I considered myself a young child. They said that if you admitted to something, they wouldn't condemn you. But I was condemned all the same; they gave me 25 years.
After a year and a half in the camps, they took off 15 of those years. Later, after I was already in the Kolyma region, another commission again took up my case, and they remitted all the remaining time on my sentence. But I wasn't allowed to return home – I still had five years deprived of rights.

Only after Stalin died was it possible to return home. So home I went, and there again I found another nightmare. No one would acknowledge me. I was still regarded as an enemy. And so I returned here to the north. I married a Russian, and so remained, for the rest of my life, here in Magadan.

* * * * *

The facts of my life can be written in just a few short lines on a piece of paper. But they do not show the person behind them, with all the years I endured – the anxieties, pains, deprivations, few joys and hunger.

At that time, it seemed that everyone cared only about themselves. I had an aunt and uncle, but they were afraid to take in my sister and myself. My sister was only seven years old, when they arrested me. Yet, none of our relatives would take us in – no one. Thankfully, other people took us, and tried to protect us.

I had a very rich boyfriend. He took care of me, and his family – imagine! – hid me. At first they did not want to put me up, but to send me to Siberia. This family probably knew when they were coming for people. They informed me, and I left with this lad. He was with me all the time.
When my parents died, all the work of the farm was on my shoulders. We had cows and horses and I did everything, even as young as I was.

Unfortunately we were constantly forced to flee from home. We weren't the only ones; everyone had to flee. The farm was left without care. The horses died, the cows were stolen, and the entire farm was destroyed little by little. Our own people began to vandalise our home; everything in the garden was pulled up by the roots; everything destroyed. We had a large bee colony. My cousin tried to take care of it but they even burnt this apiary.

The village was burnt, and everything in it. We had 40 families living in our barn, until they burnt that as well. Yes, literally everything, everything was destroyed.

We had an elderly couple take care of us. If someone came looking for us, they would answer: "We don't know where those children are." In the summer we hid in the entryway, and slept there.

* * * * *

They arrested me at home. They came at night and took me in what I had on – a linen blouse, like flax, as was usual in the village – oh, and I managed to throw on a cambric dress. They didn't even give me anything else to wear.

When they arrested me, they beat me terribly! Why? I don't know – only they know. Even now, because of those beatings, it is so painful just to think about it – it gives me nightmares.

I am terrified - they have already arrested everyone they suspect of being 'bandits' and executed them.

They demand: "Who participated in this? Speak now!"

"I don't know. I never participated in anything. I was never where you said I was."

They beat me terribly, all night long. They will not allow me to sleep.

Exhausted, we hide under the bed, like dogs, lying all night on the floor – anything to escape the beatings. Still they bully us anyway they can.

* * * * *

Then we were put in a former Jewish home. The Germans had, of course, killed all the Jews, and so their homes were standing empty. They put me in the basement there, without light. The house was derelict and full of rats. I sat there in that freezing cold basement in only a thin dress and shirt.

All night long I sat there trying to endure it all; thinking that they were probably going to shoot me, or that something even worse would happen and I would die there. I wasn't given anything to eat. I don't know, maybe it was just a test to see if I would break.

But of course, there are good people in this world. And even one of the interrogators was one of these.

He comes to me in the middle of the night. There are no windows in the basement and it is pitch black.

He comes with a candle and kefir – sour milk, as they call it – and bread.

He puts it down, I hungrily eat it all, and he leaves.

The next day, during interrogation, he says:

"They'll soon be taking you away."

"They aren't letting me go?"

"No, they aren't letting you go."

I don't know what they had on me – they never said anything around me.

This man then said to me: "Run away, run away!"

I thought: "I know that they shoot anyone who tries to run away. How could anyone give me permission to run away?" Even though I was young, I knew it would be suicidal if I ran away.

So he then asked who my relatives were and where they lived. I told him. And so he went to my godmother and informed her that I was alive, and where I was at. He was a kind person, genuine. He felt sorry for me.

He knew that very next morning they were going to move me, and so he went to my godmother and informed her that if she wanted to see me she should be there. My aunt was able to run up to me, give me some dried bread, and a scarf for my head. It was only a few fleeting seconds that we saw one another, but at least she knew I was alive.

And that was all it took. From that moment I didn't exist. I simply disappeared. My aunt and uncle, my little sister all tried to find me. They tried for more than a year, but they never could find out anything about me. They tried many times to get letters to me, but no one would ever take them.

* * * * *

I was taken, along with several other girls from our village that I didn't know, to Rovno – to prison. Here in Magadan, there had been one of my fellow countrymen, and we ended up in the same cell.

I don't know how I survived the experience of prison. They didn't bother you during the day, but at night the interrogations began. Whether they questioned you or not, you had to stand. God help you if you moved! You stood, without sleep. And if you fell asleep and fell on the floor, they would kill you.

After some time, I was put in another cell. This cell was 16 square metres in size. There was a large window, without any glass. And of course winter was coming.

Before this they had stripped my warm shirt off me in full view of everyone and locked me in this cell. I thought they were going to shoot me. I spent 11 days and nights there without food, all the while being watched through a little window in the door.

Soon the snow began. The wind would blow into the cell; snow flew in through the open window. It was cold. I had very long hair, so I would let it down, to try and cover my body with it.

It was strange seeing your death float in through an open window. I began to swell. My body expanded like a balloon. I began to lose consciousness; I simply could not hold out. I would awake and find myself on the floor. One picture kept coming to mind – crocodiles. Even today I still remember those crocodiles – crocodiles! – even though I've never seen one for real. But there in that cell, live crocodiles were crawling over me. I lay on the floor and crocodiles crawled over me.

Soon they put four more people in the cell with me. It was crowded, so that I had no place to lie down, I could only sit. My entire body hurt terribly, even my bones. Thankfully, no one beat me there. That I was able to endure those 11 days was thanks to one lady – Lidia Kryzhenovsk. This elderly lady was my cell-mate then.

We were given one cup of tea a day, along with a small spoonful of sugar, three and a half ounces of bread, and a little dab of margarine. Lidia asked the rest to give up a part of this meagre ration in order to feed me. And they used the margarine to massage my body – when the guards weren't looking of course. One would massage my hand, another my foot, and I would scream "I can't stand it!" the pain was so great. It was impossible to even touch me, but still they massaged me, and saved my life.

Before this was all over they led me down into some sort of basement. It was all white and very clean, except there were spatters of blood everywhere on the walls – probably to scare us. Maybe that was where they shot people. I thought: "It's over, this is the end." They brought me in, but didn't torture me, just left me in that nightmare of blood.

The interrogator called me in one night and said: "We were at your village, interrogated everyone, and no one would testify for you. So," he said, "the investigation is finished; it goes to trial now."

This investigator was kind. I remember his family name was Shalaev, but not his first name. If I knew he was alive and where he was today, I would certainly thank him. He was so humane. We sat all night hoping that he would touch us with his hand, even if only once. Everything that we said, he wrote down. He finished the interrogation before morning, and led me back. He was the only one who led an interrogation as he was supposed to.

Then, waiting for trial, I was again put back in a harsh and strict cell. Of course, we tried to shorten the time; to overcome the monotony of jail existence any way we could. For instance, we would sew – with thread taken from our underwear, or woollen clothes. One day they gave us some flounder to eat – of course, it was heavily salted. We used these fish bones for sewing needles. We were searched practically every night, or every other night. We would be sleeping, when suddenly before dawn, the inspector would rush in and ransack everything in the cell, searching and searching for anything and everything. We sat in silence, watching, waiting, while they yelled at us: "That's forbidden, and this is forbidden."

It is my turn on duty.

The inspector asks: "Who's on duty?" I give my name.

He answers: "To the punishment cell." He has found the fish bone needles.

So I sat in prison in a punishment cell. Thankfully, no one beat me.

Then they called me to trial.

* * * * *

Before this they gave permission for me to talk to my aunt for 10 minutes. We couldn't say very much in 10 minutes!

She kept repeating over and over: "Why don't you write, why don't you write? Not even one letter. I'm here, you know, waiting outside the prison walls." She didn't understand what kind of hell I had been in all this time.

I asked her: "Where's Olga?" My aunt said that she no longer lived with them, but with other people, that some neighbour came and took my little sister and that she now watches their cows for them.

I knew about my sister from the interrogator also. He said that my sister had been held for some time in Rovno. They had even used a little girl, seven years old, to try and get information. I thought that they had probably already exiled her, but my aunt said that she was at home, that they didn't send her anywhere. I was overjoyed at this news, and also so thankful that I could see my aunt, even for those few short moments.

* * * * *

They took us to Dnepropetrovsk, another prison. They put me to work in the basement. I prepared food, pealed potatoes at night, washed floors, cleaned up.
That was fine with me, as I wasn't hungry. I thought I would be there a long time, but within two week they sent me away again.

I'm a girl who grew up on a farm, and had never gone anywhere, and here we were travelling and travelling, one train after another. One train was with men, the next with women. Where were we going? I was homesick, wondering what more life had in store for me. I didn't see anything good in my future. I decided I wouldn't eat anything; that I would just die.

I was probably in that mood for two or three days. The supervisor noticed right away, and began to wonder. Someone told him I wasn't eating.

He called me into his berth, and asked: "What's going on?"

I don't remember now, how I answered him. But here again was a good, older man. I said my little sister was left all alone without parents, that I had never seen anything this far away from home, and I didn't even know where they were taking us.

He answered: "My dear child, we are taking you very far over the ocean." That's what he said – "over the ocean" – and I imagined something special. My uncle had gone 'over the ocean' in 1939 to America and told us all about it when I was very little. "Yes, there is a sea," he said, "where ships sail." And I thought that they were taking us overseas.

An accompanying officer showed me a photograph of me that they had. A good photo, but under my image they had written what kind of partisan I was, or some such thing. That photo had a great influence on my psyche.

He then wouldn't let me go back to the carriage with all the rest. He said: "Take a broom and sweep; sweep the corridors in the train."

How can I refuse?

I take the broom, I sweep.

The train is long and I have to sweep it from end to end. So I sweep, one female carriage after another, and then the men's carriage.

The men all give me a hard time for going into their car to sweep up.

I return to the supervisor, put the broom back in its place, don't say anything.

I don't know what else to do.

During that journey he called me in several times, saying: "Child we still have a long way to go." He encouraged me to live. How could I if I was depressed?

*   *   *   *   *

We reached Khabarovsk. There again they divided up the people into different sections; some were sent here, some were sent there. I was sent to work in the dining room. Lucky for me. I was lucky on the trip, and again in the dining car. The floors were wooden, and had to be cleaned with sand, so that they were spotless, like a mirror, glistening.

This dining carriage wasn't for the prisoners; it was just an ordinary working dining carriage. People came, ate and left. While I was working on the floor I got a big splinter in my finger. It was very painful. The splinter remained, and started to get infected. I couldn't sleep at night; I would yell out and cry. Women who didn't know anything gave all kinds of different advice. It hurt more and more, and I couldn't do anything anymore. Then it began to get better, but my finger still carries a memory of that splinter.

It was still warm as it was only September. Out of the windows we saw field upon field of cabbages, tomatoes and grain, but I didn't want to eat; I had had enough.

Upon our arrival in Naxotka, they put us all together with the common thieves and bandits, who bullied us. From there we travelled five days on the steamer *Felix Dzerzhinsk* to Magadan. Again we fell in with those imprisoned under the domestic statutes. I didn't eat anything for that long trip; the ocean was very hard to endure.

We arrived here at the bay of Nagayevo in September of 1951. Port cars stood on the shore.

Whoever was able climbed down from the deck themselves. The elderly, almost half dead, they took by car. They lined us up in rows of five and marched us barefoot the two and a half miles to our camp.

Now there are large buildings in the Nagayevo area, but then it was enclosed with barbed wire. Women were standing all along the fence, watching as we went by. I suddenly recognised one of my fellow countrymen. She yelled: "Eve! Eve!" She had already served nine years and had finished her sentence.

They took us to a camp. My friend found out which barrack I was in and brought me something to eat, along with a spoon and bowl. While I was there at the 4th kilometre camp, she helped me out.

They began to give out our assignments; who would go where. I ended up working on building projects, others at the sewing factory. I had wanted to be assigned to the sewing factory, I wanted to be able to sew, but it didn't happen. And so after they divided us up, I worked on construction. I worked so that I would be able to return to Ukraine, soon after release.

I was always thinking about my sister, and how she was. Our house was destroyed, there was nothing there; no one was waiting for me. My sister was small, and I had but one sweater. When I was released, where would I go and how? How could I help her?

* * * * *

And then they took 22 of us and sent us to Dukcha, without guards. Thus, at Dukcha I was free. We spent two years at Dukcha without guards.

When we got to Dukcha, there was to all intents and purposes, nothing there – just tents, each of which was basically a roof on a wooden platform. It was a harsh winter. To this day I don't understand why they didn't bring us any water. We used the melting snow off the roof for our tea, for washing and everything else. It was rough. We slept on these wooden floors and froze to the walls of the tents.

We were freed in 1956. At that time they were giving a northern bonus for working here. So I stayed there to receive that bonus on my earnings. And with that I could help my sister. I thought I'll earn the money in order to return home, even if all I have is this little bit to dress myself in. I returned to the building trade. At that time, one could earn good money in the building trade. And so I earned money for myself, bought a pretty dress and everything needed for the trip back to Ukraine.

Then I met my future husband.

I still hadn't left for my homeland.

We lived in a dormitory, women on the second floor, men on the third and fourth. So we got married. He was handsome and educated. He also had not had an easy life, similar to mine. I've had one great joy in my life – that my husband was such a good man. While we were young, everyone envied us. But we had many problems, him being Russian, and I Ukrainian – terrible problems.

The first time we took a trip back to Ukraine in 1957, my relatives would not accept him as they knew I had married a Russian, and things only got worse. Even my cousin would scorn me.

My brother was offended when we met; I didn't even want to go to his house.

My husband didn't understand the problem, and asked: "Why don't you visit your brother?"

I couldn't explain to him, that he was the problem.

Yet when they finally met him, they fell in love with him, probably more then I. Whenever we came again, there were never any more questions.

My younger sister also got married. She lived with her husband for two years and then divorced. She raised a son alone. When her son grew up, married and had children of his own, she went to live with them, and they took very good care of her.

At first I tried to help her, sending her all kinds of Chinese and Japanese gifts from here in the north. Then she would help me. Now she complains about how difficult it is in Ukraine again.

* * * * *

I have found many friend here like I did in the camps, and later working in the building trade. Some of them I remember by name, others only their faces, with fondness for what they did. If I have forgotten their names, may they forgive me, but I remember them in my heart, recognising their invaluable support at a difficult moment.

Yes, despite the many difficult years in the camps, I've met many good people in my life. Maybe life's lesson has given me a heightened awareness of good and evil; an understanding of unselfishness.

Today there still stands a long warehouse at the 4th kilometre point. When the freighters brought loads of cement for the construction of the city, they brought it to this warehouse and stored it there. The cement had to be bagged. The first row of sacks was laid on the ground, and then the sacks got higher and higher and higher.

Two of us were working piling these sacks of cement – they needed to be piled on the next level, but we had no strength left. There was a guard over us yelling. He would come and give us 'encouragement' with the butt of his rifle. So with the last of our strength, we had to drag yet another sack.

But then there were always people who treated me with kindness. I no longer remember the name or family of one guard, but I'm still thankful for how he helped us. Two of us were working, dragging these sacks, and he came on duty. He allowed us to rest, drink a bit of tea; he even shared with us with what food he had brought from home for himself.

Some of my friends worked in the brick factory. Prisons were everywhere. There was a camp on Yakutsk Street, in Vesoli, and in old Vesoli. I was at old Vesoli, but they were constantly taking us wherever they needed a work force.

Once we worked on the road to the invalid hospital. After work we had to gather up a store of wood to heat the barracks. And we had to go through deep snow, and my felt boots were worn out completely. Still I had to look for some sort of stumps or sticks. The young and the old, all had to find wood, and haul it all the way back to the hospital. They didn't care about our woes.

Not far from Magadan, in a swamp, was a field where they had grown turnips. In the autumn they made us gather them up. We worked in the rain getting soaked to the skin. After cleaning up we returned home at the end of the day. Some had hidden the roots of these turnips under their armpits, so as to keep a little food for themselves. But when we went by the guard station, the supervisor searched us, practically stripping us of all our clothes. Those who were found with those turnip roots were put in lock down.

I had a friend Anna while in camp. She had been freed earlier, when I was just being sentenced. There was no bedding. Anna had moved to an old barracks that was near the old cemetery. She occupied the little kitchen and put her bed there.

She always visited me in the camp, so the guards knew her. She would go to the man on duty and asks him a question. The girls were watching for this moment. Anna tossed us some bread: it was freshly baked and delicious; we ate it all up.

Anna knew the guards, and to whom it was possible to go up to and ask. There were those guards who would immediately shoot you.

She really helped me a lot. Then she moved away, and we wrote to each other for a long time.

Many people helped me. At times I didn't even know who it was. Not long ago, a woman told me: "I think my husband liked you." I didn't know what she was talking about. She told me that her husband when he left home for work always asked her to set something aside for him to eat.

When I worked on the building sites, we painted, did finishing, plastered and everything else. We also worked on window frames, which needed to be assembled, sealed, painted and ready for installation. And several times it happened that arriving at this work, there was bread, margarine, or sausage left for me. This turns out to have been her husband who left it for me then. And only now I found out who gave me these gifts.

Here's a quite different relationship. We were led on foot from work back to the camp, in columns of five through rain and mud. And once beyond the bus stop, all the way for the next two and a half miles, they could make us 'hit the dirt' whenever they wanted. The guards were particularly conscientious in fulfilling this duty when it was muddy. Often by the time we got to our camps we had already been forced to 'hit the dirt' six times. Of course, we hadn't broken any rules; they just wanted to force us to lie on the road in the mud. God forbid that someone would toss something to us, a can or something. God forbid if you were to bend over. If you broke formation that would be it, you were punished.

* * * * *

I would constantly pray silently and in my heart ask God to give me strength, especially in the difficult times. We girls also prayed together in the camp. We always managed to celebrate Easter, but of course, with lots of lookouts. Wherever I went, I went with God. Some people say that he doesn't exist. But I know that the Lord God always was, and is, and always will be with me.

All my life, since my earliest childhood, and to the end of our days, my family has lived close to God.

My father was a very religious person. In our village the road to the church was visible to all. Papa went to church every day. He was very punctual. This was his character, to be constant and exact. He served as an indisputable stop-clock in the village. Few people had clocks back then, but villagers would know the time by my father. They would see my father returning from church, and say: "There goes Roman, it's time for lunch."

They also taught us religion in school in those days, and that has stayed with me all my life. Now I always hold the name of the Lord God in my heart with thanksgiving.

* * * * *

How I now long for Ukraine. When I lay down to rest, I picture every little detail in my mind, every friend, my parents and family; I remember everything. These memories have become very sharp lately.

Once, there were foreigners who had come to Ukraine; they came to visit the graves of their ancestors. They were already old people. I figured they would return home where they had a good life, but they remained in Ukraine. And now as I remember them I think I need to do the same thing. If only I could return to Ukraine!

Oh, how I want to return!

The last time I was in Ukraine was with my husband in 1988. Now I live so simply, so poorly. I never imagined it would be like this. I had worked so much, and for so long in construction, I thought I would be able to care for myself in my old age. I thought I had everything here. I was earning money, and I was even healthy. Why go back home, there's nothing in that village, that remote place?

Now I think that I made a mistake. I would be home with my own people, with my relatives with whom I could talk, heart to heart. Almost every one of my friends who has had the opportunity has left. And while there are still several friends left here, I can only share my cares with them only when we meet in church.

I'm shut up in these four walls and don't have anyone to talk to. People sell their homes and leave. Other people come, but you don't even know them. I used to love company very much. I always had many people coming to visit. That's all over, now there is no one. Yes, I'm ashamed of how I live now.

I've been rehabilitated. I can come and go like everyone else, without worry. When I went home to Ukraine before, the community representative, or someone else from the government, would come to me. They knew I was a former prisoner, and at first ordered me to be gone within 24 hours. But I had already been rehabilitated, and so I would tell them: "I have the right to live anywhere – even in Moscow if I choose."

All the ladies would say to me: "You are really bold, Eve."

I would reply: "I have all the documents with me, and he seemed to indicate that I couldn't live in this village. I can live in Moscow if I want."

But what do I have to show them now? Life is full of pain. Even for our children, life is all difficulties, and will probably be so till death. Enemies are everywhere. A tribunal of the NKGB judged me then. They decided everything then.

The meeting of the former repressed in the Church of the Nativity is not just to talk about the past; it's an affirmation of the strength of our spirit that enabled us to live through all of that. I like these gatherings. Every month they try to show or tell us something new. It's not just a party. These meetings help us to overcome the feeling that we are no longer needed by anyone. They give us hope, and while a person lives, he very definitely needs hope.

Anna Ivanovna Zhuk

Born:	April 5th 1930
Where:	Berctsk, Ivanovsk region
Country:	Belarus
Arrested:	1949
Sentence:	25 years hard labour, plus 5 years deprived of rights
Released:	May 1956
Rehabilitated:	1956

THERE WERE FOUR CHILDREN IN OUR FAMILY, three girls and a boy. When they arrested me, they also took the others, sending us to the Urals and to Perm. Our entire family was exiled. My brother and one sister died there. Only one sister survived.

It was a very difficult time. All throughout the war, we lived in German-occupied territory. They took everything we had, forcing us to live in a mud hut. Everything around us was bombed out and destroyed. The bombing was constant, we were constantly taking cover. They were very difficult times. I was only able to finish fourth grade, two years in a Polish school, and two years in a Russian school. Then they arrested me, and I ended up in a prison camp, a camp with a harsh regime.

They first took me in 1949, but soon let me go. They arrested me for the second time on September 15th 1950. This time they didn't let me go, and from that moment on I was a prisoner. My trial only began in 1951, and of course there was no evidence, as they had nothing on me. Since I was still underage when they arrested me, they had to bide their time. At the inquest, they mocked me terribly, taking me at 6pm for interrogation and only finishing at 9am; it went on all night long. And they beat me. Oh how they beat me… kicking me in the chest with their boots till I was black and blue. They taunted me terribly. They taunted me often. They were worse

217

than Germans, they were like wild animals. That is what I can see before my eyes, I don't even like to think about it, it's very difficult.

But even among these animals, there were good people. I remember one of the investigators – Zhuravlev was his name. He was questioning me while someone was sitting near the door writing, and he said: "Listen, someone's coming, stand quickly." He was a good investigator; he never once laid a finger on me. But others are terrible to remember.

And what was so terrible, was that they took you during the night, only returning you in the morning, and then it was impossible to sleep – the supervisor saw to that. In the cell we all lived and slept on the concrete floor. They tormented us as much as possible. It was almost too much to endure.

So I was arrested on September 15th 1950 and went to trial on March 16th 1951 in the city of Pinsk. I received a sentence of 25 years of hard labour, including five years without rights. I was an enemy of the people! I was accused of betraying the Motherland. What could I do with only a fourth grade education? How could I defend myself? Even educated people stood no chance of saving themselves.

Once they took you, they wouldn't let you go, they would find something, make up something against you; literally make up something from nothing. And I hadn't lived long under the Russians, but had lived mainly under Polish rule. I could barely even speak Russian! Then the war began and we had to survive that as well. When the war ended, the hard labour began. I had been given my sentence and they said: "We are taking you where there are polar bears".

And they did.

* * * * *

From Belarus they took me by stages to Moscow and from there by long steps to Novosibirsk. These stages went on and on. They only fed us if and when they happened to have some food. From Novosibirsk they took me to Nakhotka, to the port of Vanino. I remember that there was a famous singer, Ruslanova, with us there. She had been a celebrity during the war, and even after. Everyone would become very quiet when she sang softly, from her corner. But she didn't sail with us from Nakhotka, and I never saw her again. I can't say if she was ever in Magadan or not.

We waited 20 days in Nakhotka, and then they loaded us on the freighter *Felix Dzerzhinski*, and we sailed for seven days and nights. In Nakhotka, they had said for some reason: "Don't worry; you won't be under guard there or anything." We wanted to believe it, but didn't know what to think. But, oh, when we arrived…

We were met by a heavily armed guard, with weapons and dogs. It was terribly frightening. We were lined up and marched to the sanitary inspection station. There they inspected us, washed us, dressed us in something and gave us our numbers. I was A-88. We were then marched to a barrack two and a half miles farther on and from there made to work building a road to the invalid home, but that didn't last long – less than a month.

When we arrived at this barrack, they again began to form us into ranks, calling our number and lining us up. Those who had the longer sentences, that is those sentenced to hard labour, were sent off to Butugichag – the uranium mine. I worked the mines there two years. We did everything we were forced to do, hauled ore, drilled, cut lumber. They beat every last drop of strength from us. The few survivors from Butugichag – and they were barely human – were taken by truck to Bakxanku, and from there to Xinxanzhy. Again we were sent to the mines. Every day, we would go and someone would fall asleep; or the mines would collapse. We could not endure the unbearable work. Of the girls alone, very few survived to be freed.

In September, near the enclosure but beyond the fence, the low bush cranberries were ripening. But they wouldn't let us gather them, saying: "Why do you need berries?" If you even reached for these berries, you would be shot from the tower, leaving the berries in your hand. That was how they rewarded us. It's very difficult to think back on these things; very difficult.

In the camp, there was a female doctor who pulled three healthy teeth from my mouth, saying: "What difference does it make? You'll be dead before you finish your sentence!" My nose was frostbitten; my gums were so sore from the cold; I had scurvy. This doctor put leeches on my gums.

Everything depended on the person, and people are different. That's how things are.

And then this happened to me: I fell ill. They sent me to work in the mines, helping two civilian surveyors; one was a woman by the name of Marika. She had only three more days left of her sentence. I was so small and skinny that they sent me up a shaft with a tape measure. I felt it begin to give way, and shouted: "Run!" But they thought I was just feeling dizzy. They called up: "Climb down slowly!" And at that moment, everything collapsed. I was up top and was buried to my waist. Marika was under me. The rocks ruptured her spleen, and she died where she was standing. We waited from morning until evening. When there was roll call in camp and we didn't show up, they sent someone looking for us and dug us out.

They brought me to Magadan, to a military hospital for some reason. The doctor, a colonel, treated me very well. He said: "I don't care if she betrayed the Motherland or not, I'm a doctor and I'll treat her." And so he treated me. I was all covered in casts. Unfortunately they didn't keep me there long. As soon as the casts were off they sent me as an invalid up the road to where there was an invalid home. And as soon as I started to walk a little bit, they sent me back to the camp, to sweep, wash dishes, other 'light work'.

But I didn't remain there long either. They sent me off to work on a building site. They weren't allowed to leave those with long sentences on light work for as long as they pleased. We heard all the time: "You can die just as well in the camps."

* * * * *

I remember how we were building a children's home near the theatre and a little hill. First we dug a trench. One of the girls suggested that we eat our ration of bread together, first one, then the other. "You come here," she said. "We'll eat one ration, and then the other." I answered, "There's a little sun on this side; you come over here." No sooner had I said this but the trench collapsed on them. That was it… she was buried and died. Only one Lithuanian woman was left alive and her pick was buried.

It wasn't the first time that I looked death in the face. And so I just can't think about all that, it becomes so difficult.

Then I had a serious heart attack. I was only 25 years old. I lay in the hospital in Dukcha for almost a year. I was saved by the generosity of people – my friends and co-patriots. They brought me honey and sugar. It was forbidden to give me medicine. I had breathed as much uranium dust as I could. Medicine only made me worse. But people saved me.

There was a doctor in that hospital, Maria Fedorovna, who was a good woman and a good doctor. She once dropped into my ward and said: "I'm going to give you a shot to calm you down." But there was little that could upset me anymore. Everything seemed the same; everything I had gone through made no difference to me – even the heart attack. And the 25 year sentence, five without rights, was considered a life sentence. So nothing was important to me anymore. But she gave me the shot anyway. I looked up and several officers came in. There was a colonel among them. They came up to me and announced: "We've taken 15 years off your sentence of hard labour, and the five years without rights!"

The doctor laughed: "Now you can't die, you've almost completed your sentence!"

I was returned to the camp in Dukcha. I only had two year left to serve. The head of the camp said that I would go even before that.

In May of 1956, a commission came from Moscow including our KpCh commandant, the commandant of the Shevchenko camp, and the commandant. They said: "All right girls, gather round, get yourselves in order, you'll be leaving."

* * * * *

They bring us to Magadan.

The commission meets us in an office. They lead us there under guard, one by one. Lord, we go there with our hands tied behind us, yet already almost free. Yet, we have no idea what awaits us.

The guards – thankfully! – encourage us, saying: "Don't be afraid, girls, everything will be all right. If they say to you: 'Sit, citizen' – consider yourself free."

They called me last, as my last name – Sereda – started with an 's'. They began by asking everything anew, who was I, where was I from, for what was I accused, and I answered what I knew.

They talked in such a reassuring tone, but then we were used to that. They then led me to another dark room, and I sat and waited while they consulted.

They call me back and say: "Well, sit, citizen."

"Well," I think, "that's that."

But they ask further: "You had on a yellow ring when they arrested you. Was it gold?"

I answer: "I don't know, Grandma died, and my family gave it to me."

They answer: "It was gold, and it should be returned to you."

I don't need a ring anymore; I don't need anything.

Of course, it was never returned. But my parents did get some money returned to them. How could a ring make up for the fact that they had sent me from my home, that I had lived for so many years without a home, or food, or work, or any rights?

* * * * *

When I was free, they gave me a paper saying that I had been condemned without sufficient cause. And within five days they gave me a clean passport – one that did not mention my past –plus a paper stating that my work in the camps will count as service, though not towards retirement. But perhaps that was for the best because if these 10 years were spread out over my entire work record, then my pension might be even less. Thus do the laws work against us.

They released 25 of us at one time – our entire brigade. But only four of us received full rights, me – a Lithuanian! – Galia Yurcunyak, Galia Shporok and Eve Onofreichuk. The others only had their sentences removed, that was all. They told us that everyone had been sentenced without evidence. I was freed on May 6th 1956, on Good Friday, just before Easter.

To be able to go about without guards – such joy!

I started out living with sick deportees, and almost starved again. I remember how once some other exiles from the Baltics treated us to all kinds of food – fish and even Champagne! Yes, they gave Champagne to starving people – can you imagine it? – even to the girls! It was the first time I had ever tasted it. I only remember that I clearly recognised everything and understood everything, but that my legs wouldn't cooperate. There was an older man, Yogan, who very much wanted me to go out with his son. That's probably why they treated us like they did.

Then an acquaintance, Kostia Punchuk, took me in to live with her family. But I soon married. I also continued to worked right there where I was, in the building trade; painting and hanging wallpaper. I worked there all the time until retirement in 1984.

I always worked hard. We would have young children come to work right from high school or trade school, and the boss always put them with us more experienced workers for training, and still he would say: "You watch out, be careful with her, she's an enemy of the people."
I'm a patient person, and always keep quiet, but all the same I had to endure that as well.

Throughout my entire life any one could belittle me like that. Not only in the camps – there you have to take care of yourself – but after the camps as well, so many times I heard such insults! It was difficult and painful. Even now, it still happens, that people judge and insult us. That's all you need to hear. That person is, perhaps, worse than I, yet he sits there and judges. It's not very nice.

I worked long, hard years and endured all kinds of things. I even fell from the fifth floor and somehow lived, thanks be to God. I said that my God saved me. He always saved me. Even the doctors said as much: "You were flying, fell on asphalt, but God must have held you up." Of course, I cracked my skull, had my kidney removed, burst my eardrums, and other fractures, whatever could be, and yet I lived. The Lord always upheld me.

I'm from a believing, Orthodox family. Everyone believed then. Even in the camps, at every trial or depravation, God did not abandon us. Even in secret, we practiced our faith, celebrating Easter and other feasts. The Lord God has always lived in my heart.

* * * * *

I met my husband while in the camps. We were sometimes sent to work on communal projects, when we were on sick leave, washing vegetables or building cold storage sheds, and we met there. He worked as an officer of the sea port. He was 10 years older than I was. He had a higher education in physics and mathematics. And he endured all the jokes about his little girl with good humour.

We were married in 1956 and lived together exactly 20 years. He died in 1976. We had a good life together. We respected and honoured each other. We have one son. When our son was in eighth grade, my husband said to him: "Your mother was in the camps, you should know about that, and whether I am living or not, you must never reproach her for that, never!" But I could never ask him about his past because as soon as we started to talk about his family, his eyes would fill with tears.

So even now I don't know for sure. Maybe they too were sent into exile, I don't know. He wasn't among the repressed himself. I do know that there were four children in his family, two boys and two girls. One brother died near Lviv in the war. His sister Nadya was a doctor, and also died in the war. His youngest sister, Olga, was sent by the Germans to Germany in 1928.

And his mother...

When the Germans entered Poltav (he himself was from Poltav, and fought there) he stopped in at home and his mother was baking bread. Suddenly, they started bombing, and he ran out of the house. At that moment, a bomb fell on the house and everyone inside was killed.

His younger sister wrote to us from Canada in 1957. But my husband reported that, as he should have, to the KGB, and all correspondence ceased. The times were like that. Everyone was afraid.

Now my grandson tries to find someone through the internet. We, of course don't need anything, but my one son says, perhaps, somewhere out there is just one related soul. I have two grandsons, they are both wonderful. One grandson works in a music school. The other was in the young pioneers, then served in the military and is now in the reserves. He served in the navy in Kamchatka. When he returned home, couldn't find work and so re-enlisted.

My son had this happen to him: he applied to the aviation academy after serving in the army. Someone from my work place wrote on a certificate that his mother betrayed the Homeland. This was 1977. She wrote this and didn't say anything to us. Perhaps, if I had known that she had done that, I could have gone to the KGB and corrected it. We only found out when they rejected him. It was too late to shout. But my son survived, he finished at our Magadan institute.

* * * * *

Only in 1984 did I leave on a trip for the first time. Before that I wasn't able to do so, not for lack of money, but because I wasn't allowed. I didn't want to fall apart, there were no relatives left, no one waiting there; only very bitter memories. Still, in 1984, my sister and I went to see where we had spent our childhood. There is still the most beautiful forest there. We travelled to Xatyn, not far from Minsk. We visited an army base there and handed out notebooks, books, pens and apples to the soldiers. In Brest we placed roses at the memorial. We tried so hard to keep it together, but our nerves could not endure it. We broke out in a nervous rash all over our body, and started to have heart problems. When we went to the clinic, we were not accepted; we were foreigners. That's how it was, the younger ones didn't know anything, and no one needed us. And to whom would we explain it? After that bitter experience, we decided not to travel again. Our hearts could not bear it.

In 1999, I suffered another serious heart attack. I fell in my garden, and lost consciousness. And again the Lord helped me; the Lord and people around me. I have many good people in my life. A good friend always comes and visits. We've been friends for 30 years, and we never leave the other in difficulty. And I have good grandsons, and a wonderful son. I never heard a harsh word from him; he always called me dear Mama.

That's how it was; both the good and the bad. Praise God. I thank God for every day of life; especially for my children and grandchildren. I am so proud of them.

Anastasia Semenovna Lexnik

Born:	November 1st 1928
Where:	Lukva, Ivano-Frankovsk region
Country:	Ukraine
Arrested:	June 1st 1947
Sentence:	10 years hard labour
Released:	Beginning of 1955

WE ARE PURE-BLOODED UKRAINIANS through my grandfather and great-grandfather. We were always farmers, but we were capable of any trade. One of my ancestors even built a church. There were six children in our family, one brother, and the rest of us were girls. Mama had prayed to the blessed Mother asking to be given at least one son. Our Peter suffered greatly under the Soviets.

He was arrested on December 6th 1946 along with an older sister, Eustasia. They arrested them in the middle of the night, at three am. They arrested many others that night. They were able to bully them. This just destroyed our family. But then, people can say the same thing everywhere in Ukraine.

They arrested me on June 1st 1947, the feast of the Blessed Trinity – a major feast day for our Church. The entire family was in church as we always enjoyed being there. There was such beauty all around the church – lilacs, jasmine, peonies and roses everywhere. And it was like that in every garden too, such was our faith. Later the cherries would bloom, and the apples, and red and blackcurrants, which we called *puryshkami*. Everything was in bloom. Our dear mother Ukraine was full of such beauty, especially when everything was flowering with such sweet smells – yes, such indescribable beauty.

We went to church that morning not suspecting anything. O Good Lord, the KGB agents surrounded the church, and then stormed in, stopping the service. What difference was it to them, if it was the feast of the Holy Trinity? They yelled at the priest: "Stop, how long will this continue?" They started to force everyone outside. There were two exits from the church. They forced everyone through only one. They had a list. Anyone on the list was taken and put on the side. They took 26 people like that. Then they searched inside the church again, to be sure no one was hiding there. The beautiful flowers around the church were ruined by the machine guns. At home they broke the locks, and ransacked everything.

Of course, they didn't find anything – there was nothing to find! Still they forced us to sign some sort of paper.

They took us straight to the local council, where they also brought those who weren't at the church. No one was hiding; who, after all, knew they were coming? The village was occupied until the next morning. They didn't allow anyone in from the other villages – my friend tried. He had gone to the church to meet with me, and they arrested him and two other farmers. They brought them to the council too and interrogated them about who they were, why they were there and where they were from. They had to send someone back to their village for their documents, to find out if they really were who they said they were. And he was the secretary of the local timber industry! They eventually let him go, after much interrogation. He endured so much for nothing.

A truck arrived with dogs and machine guns, and they loaded us on to it. I remember how the head KGB agent, tapping his pockets, boasted: "Ah, today was a great success! I've earned a lot of money for today's work, gathering all the troublemakers from this village."

* * * * *

They took us to Solotvino, and the next day we were moved on to Ivano-Frankovsk. The inquest continued all the way into the autumn. It was already cold by the time they moved us, in stages, to Lviv. There we were held for some time. Eventually we were sent to the north, to Komi USSR. We worked on the railway bed there. They told us it was Vorkuta and Comsomolsk. I remember when we were working on that project, how planes – some quite large – would fly over us, one after the other. Then, through the convoy, we found out that they had photographed us and written an article on how the young communist workers were building a road. The guards were laughing at us; "Did you know you weren't prisoners, but young communist workers?"

That's how it seemed to outsiders. But in fact it was quite different, as anyone who was repressed knows. I don't even want to remember the inhuman conditions, the harsh guards, the unbearable work, the starvation rations, the work – it's so difficult.

Later they transferred us to the Irkutsk region, to a special camp in Taishet. Here we could only send two letters a year. It was an extremely harsh regime, although I can't say anything personally about the punishment system. I remember one morning though, the brigade leader came to our door early and announced: "Girls, we are leaving the 'zone'." One lady from Latvia was so happy, saying: "Get up girls, we have to go! Stalin ordered, we don't have a choice. Why bother?" Someone reported her and she was thrown into the punishment cell, where she sat starving.

In Irkutsk, we worked on different projects, such as digging foundations. Of course we had to dig the foundations by hand. In order to haul out the dirt, we had to cut steps in the side of the foundation. Whoever was at the very bottom would place a load on the first step, and the next person would lift it to the next step, and so on to clear out the foundation. Imagine how much dirt had to be removed like that for a large foundation. And we had a quota to fill.

We also worked cutting lumber. The trees were very tall, like the columns of grand buildings. We worked loading logs onto trucks. All the work was very hard; it's difficult to even think about it. I worked there till Armistice Day.

* * * * *

My whole family – all our relatives, all the children, too! – was arrested and exiled to Siberia in that terrible year of 1947. They arrested me on June 1st and before the October holidays had come around they had arrested the rest of my family – my sisters and parents – and exiled them as well. And not only my immediate family, but my relatives from the Omsk region, the Vasisski region and the village of Imshagal. At that time there were already Cubans, Cherksi, and Volga Germans living there. They had already

231

survived until that time. The young Germans were very good people who worked hard.

I was 18 years old when they took me, and 24, going on 25 when I was freed. I endured that punishment for seven and a half years.

* * * * *

When I was freed, I immediately asked for permission to return to my homeland. They gave me permission, but didn't want to let me go right away. They sent us to the Mordovski region instead. They explained that we were free, but would have better luck in the Mordovski region. They also placed us in camps there, but there wasn't the hard, difficult work. But there were tree stumps to remove, and so right away they sent me to clear stumps. We lived in nice barracks – they even had glass in the windows! It was very pretty. We had a commandant over us. They gathered us all together, just like on the trip from Moscow, then they gave us the final certificates. We worked there for a month and a half, and of course, now we did not have to report for work at 6am, but later than that. But still, though they couldn't herd us like sheep any more, they still gave us a quota for how many of those stumps we had to dig out. They gave us a section and we had to clear all the stumps and roots. Some places were easy and others were more difficult, if the trees had deep roots. It was hard work, but we managed to clear those stumps.

Then the commandant came with his list of who was to go on which train carriage for the trip to Moscow. He led us barefoot to the station, but now we didn't have to march in rows, but just walked as we wanted to, and the commandant didn't even yell at us! Arriving at the station, the train was already there, and the commandant let us board. The carriages were even passenger carriages, and they served tea, just as you might imagine!

But of course, we didn't feel that we were really free, and didn't believe it, as there was a convoy behind us – just another convoy taking us somewhere. It had been many long years always feeling that I was being trailed by a convoy. I had already been a prisoner for seven and a half years. We all felt dismayed and not at all at peace, not believing that we were free. We expected someone to yell "Attention!" and command us to get off the train.

At last we reached Moscow, and from there travelled to Omsk. I was the only one going north, except for two ladies from Latvia going to their families. All the rest boarded trains to western Ukraine, to Fankovsk and to Lviv.

And in Omsk, I went to my relatives.

I went to see my relatives in the village of Talovk. It was a village of 12 huts, full of unhappy migrants. The cow barns were farther off, four and a half miles away. Except for a couple of horses and these people, no one else was there, except those Cubans, Czechs, and Germans who were brought there earlier, and Ukrainians. The Cubans were already free at that time to come or go as they pleased, but of course none of them wanted to leave. They had already built homes, had cattle and pigs and other farm animals, and were surviving. They had been there several generations, and their parents were buried there, and the younger ones felt that this was already their home.

Soon, my younger sister, Vasilia, found me there. They admitted her to the communal farm and she came. I immediately asked: "Is Mother living? Is Father?" We never referred to our parents informally, as we were brought up to treat our parents with the highest respect. She answered: "Yes, Mother is still alive, as is Father, only his legs hurt and he has trouble walking."

My family, they endured so much. When they were taken, they were given 20 minutes to collect their things. But what could they take with them? Why, nothing! A lot of pain and suffering came from this. When I at last came to their village, my dear little Mama walked a long way to come and meet me. Oh, I can't even think about it, or describe what a reunion it was! In Omsk, I lived with relatives about two years. I still worked cutting timber, as I refused to join the communal farm. They didn't look too kindly on me for that, but I didn't care, I wasn't afraid anymore. I went to the lumber region, to Pixovi. Many people from our village chose to work there, especially the younger ones, as the old people couldn't go far. My father, on the other hand, was forced to work, as he was a carpenter. They set him to work repairing sleighs, as it was winter. In the summer, he worked on the homes.

Nor did they leave Mama alone, even though she was old. They made her weed flax, then gather and spin it. It was so difficult for her, her hands swelled up so much that she wasn't able to do anything. And then my sister got on the village council – she had been in the army and was able to throw those wicked people around. She said: "I work day and night, I'm practically supporting the whole farm myself; you do the spinning yourself." And at last they left my dear Mama alone. Father still had to work, but then whenever they received a delivery of cloth, he received two or three yards and so we were able to make our own clothes.

There were good people there who advised me as to where to write about my parents' assets which they had lost when they were exiled. I wrote lots of letters, and replies came from Omsk and Moscow. The replies always came to the commandant, and every month I still had to register with them. I also wrote to Kiev, because Moscow said it was Kiev that liquidated us. But of course, Kiev said it was all Moscow's responsibility.

At that time, the regional commandant from Vasis came every month to register us and to be sure we hadn't run off. That was simple life in the Soviet Union. Even after we were freed, we still lived as if we were in a prison camp. So the commandant would come and inform us if a decision had come about leaving. He would always forcefully request that we help with the harvest, saying: "You will go, we, of course will provide your documents and let you go. I'll bring the documents with me – the next time I come."

That was how it was. I could leave the sawmill any time I wanted, I could quit, but my sister had to help with the harvest on the communal farm. Only when the brigade leader declared the fields all cleared did we receive our final permission to leave. We gathered up everything there was. Yes, Lord, what little there was! We were given a pass and we left along with several other people. This was the spring, March of 1957. I only remember that we arrived home in April. I don't remember the date, but it was almost Easter.

* * * * *

It was difficult to reach Omsk. We travelled by trucks and even bulldozers until we found a car which, for a price, brought us to Omsk. The driver took us straight to the train station. There, we all bought tickets, Father, Mother, my younger sister Vasilis and I. We were heading home.

From Omsk we travelled to Moscow, where we had to change trains; from there it was an easy trip to Frankovsk, and then to Stanislav.

As soon as we got off the train, mother and father fell to their knees, and kissed the holy soil of home. Dear God, how they had wanted to return! Even in Omsk they would cry for home. Father often sat smoking his pipe with tears flowing from his eyes wondering when we would ever get out of there. Mama wrung her hands, and would sob uncontrollably. Eternal Rest to you, my dear Mama!

Of course, we had once had a home and everything we needed there in Ukraine. Now we had to live in a shack, a former stable – we chased the horse out and settled my parents there. Lord, what is there to say? So many tears, so much suffering, so much persecution, so much injustice we had to endure! I don't like remembering all this so I'll just be quiet.

And how was our old home when they returned? A garrison had been stationed on our land such that their kitchen was in our garden. We had a large barn, where we used to keep horses. The shed for the cows and pigs was where they kept their horses. Of course, since we weren't there, they had simply done as they pleased. There were now three garrisons in our village. So everyone just had to adjust to the new reality.

Even the priest's home had been burnt down. The priest had been my father's friend since they were one year old. The priest's name was Ivan, and his family name was Tishber. He was from somewhere in Galich. When he finished at the seminary, they sent him to our village. He would often come to our house.

They burnt his house down because they had wanted him to become Orthodox, but he refused, saying: "I was born and baptised a Ukrainian Greek Catholic; I lead the Divine Service. How can I change?" He flatly refused. They wanted to throw him out of the village, but he was not young either. So he begged to be allowed to stay in one half of our house, so that he could remain near the church. The decision as to whether or not he was a criminal was slow in coming from Kiev, but at last they decided he could stay – and that he could live with us. He was so happy. He even ended up dying right there in our house. And we carried him to his grave. That was our life – it was very difficult. It's difficult to even think about it.

Our family was very religious and was highly respected in the village. Do you know how many people gathered when we returned? After all our family was very large, with many kinfolk there and in the neighbouring villages. They let everyone know that we were returning, and they came to

235

meet us. We found out all the news – who had married and so on – from our cousins and distant relatives. Seeing that my parents were already old, many thought that they would probably not be able to return. But thanks be to God, they did return. I had personally begged God, innumerable times, to allow them to return to their home and live but three years in their hut under the hazelnut trees. And God gave them not three, but 18 years. There was no greater joy for me than that my parents returned to their home.

* * * * *

I ended up here in Magadan, because my brother, Peter, had to serve a seven year sentence here in the Dneprovski camp. My husband was also sent to that camp. They were there at the same time, but didn't know each other. And of course, the camp was far off. My brother suggested I come here, and he would find work for me, even if only in the sewing factory. So I did. I came to Magadan in 1958. I spent about a year with my parents, and then moved to Magadan to be near my brother. He had married, and already had a daughter, Nina.

I began to work, made many friends, married, and had two children. And so I stayed in Magadan. I lived there 33 years, surviving from each year to the next. I worked in the sewing factory, and from there retired.

* * * * *

When we worked in Taishet, we wore a number on our blouse and jumper. My number was A-661. This abasement was the worst thing for me – that and knowing I could be killed any minute. Good Lord, don't let anyone say anything against another, they could shoot you without warning! We were lined up, surrounded by dogs, and warned: "Take a step out of line to the right or to the left and you will be shot without warning." It was the same on the work projects. God forbid anyone should step outside of the 'zone', even put a foot out and you would be shot instantly. And it happened so many times, people were simply shot dead. Indeed, every step was terrible; they ordered 'Down!' and, mud or no mud, everyone had to lay with their faces to the ground. Rarely was there a calm and carefree day. We were threatened every minute. I can't remember even one normal day. Even when we had free days, they still ordered us out to pick up trash from the yards where the supervisors lived. They could do that whenever they pleased – winter and summer, day in and day out. Yes, humiliation on humiliation; that was probably the worse.

What helped me to survive those seven years in prison? It was God's will, His strength, and the Holy Spirit. Whatever I did, and wherever I went, I constantly prayed. I would walk along in formation and I only prayed; prayer was all I had. That is what saved me – nothing else could – only the Lord God, and his strength. And of course, my dear sweet Mama prayed for me, kneeling or with her face to the ground, begging that God would protect me. I had seen how she prayed for her children when they arrested Peter and Eustasia before me. My two older sisters, Marge and Evdox, were also exiled to Siberia, one to Tyomensk, the other to Kemerov. No one was left in the village; no one was allowed to stay. Only father, mother and my youngest sister Vasilia could stay; all the rest were sent to different places.

They did this intentionally – not only me and my family, but many, many families were split up and sent to different places. I thought we would never see each other again. But, thanks be to God, we were able to see each other again, and in our home town! Most importantly, we have photographs of us together again. My daughter Irina has them in Khabarovsk. I have two children, two daughters. One is here, married, living in Magadan. The other is in Khabarovsk. I am very grateful to God for my children. They are very good to me; they studied well at school, graduated from university and are working. And I have a very good husband. I can't complain about him. He doesn't smoke or drink, and we were always close. He was also from Ukraine, only from a different part, from Drouobichsk.

And I have found our Church here through Fr Michael. I consider myself lucky to be able to go to church. It is a great joy for me. I had gone to the Orthodox church often, but it became too difficult for me to stand. Here it's easier for me. I can hear every word that is spoken, and know what they are talking about. How precious are these prayers to me, O Lord! Thank you for everything. I will never stop thanking Him.

Anton Vasilevich Voloshin

Born: 1898
Arrested: November 23rd 1937
Accusation: Spying and betrayal of
                Motherland.
Sentence: Execution by firing squad
Carried out: December 8th 1937
Rehabilitated: February 6th 2002

As told by his daughter, Evgenia Antonovna Voloshin, pictured above

I, EVGENIA VOLOSHIN, WAS BORN ON JANUARY 1st 1928, in the city of Dnipropetrovs'k. My parents had two children, me and my brother, who was four years older than I. Mama didn't work, but Papa worked as a driver for the local administration, chauffeuring a small car. We were a middle class family, not rich, but not poor either. We lived simply in a large communal building. Formerly it was the home of some rich landowner. When it was taken over by the Soviets, it was given to the local authorities. There in that large home, they placed 17 families, and there I spent my childhood.

I also went to school there, but was only able to finish fifth grade, before the war started. I studied in a Russian school, as there were more Russian schools than Ukrainian ones. I especially remember my first teacher, a German lady by nationality, Vera Adolphovna Pelshay. Overall, I have fond memories of my childhood. When my father came home from work, I always went running to meet him. Our house stood in the middle of the block, and as soon as he appeared around the corner, I would run to him and he would catch me, lifting me to his shoulders, and carry me home. I carry such memories with me.

241

My parents were very good. They never argued in front of us, but perhaps they did when we weren't around. Around us they were friendly, wonderful parents. They did everything for us, their children. Papa never punished us, but loved us, his dear children, very much. Mama loved us too, as one would expect of a mother, but not every child had a Papa such as we had. I certainly can't fault my parents for anything. Practically every summer Papa would try and rent a summer home in the country. So when my brother had vacation, he would rent a country house for us, with a little stream nearby and a little garden, where we could sit or gather apples. I went swimming everyday. That was how we spent our summers. Papa would join us every Sunday, as at that time, he had to work six days a week, with the 6th, 12th, 18th, 24th and 30th being days off. That was the law.

So he arrived on August 17th 1937, in the evening, and said to Mama: "We're going home".

"What already?"

"Yes, there was a disturbance in the city, something strange, we're going home."

We spent the 18th together and then returned to the city. We gathered up our things, and went home.

They came for him on the 23rd. He had a feeling that he should come for us a week earlier than usual. If he hadn't I don't know what would have happened. After all, no one knew where we were, and no one would have been able to contact us when they came for him, or say where they took him or what had happened to him. And Mama only had a few *kopecks* left for food, which wouldn't have lasted long.

They came for him between four and five in the morning. I was nine years old at the time. I only know that we were all woken up; there were two soldiers in the room and two witnesses. They always had witnesses with them. They ransacked the entire home. And what were they looking for? That's yesterday's news, as they say.

After ransacking the house, they then took Papa. Of the 17 families in that home, they arrested the director and his wife, plus another of our neighbours. In all four people were taken from our building.

Mama, of course, started making the rounds of the stations, trying to find out where he was, what happened to him and why. No one would ever take a message for him. But still she continued to try to get a message to him.

In another month and a half, maybe two, the same ones from the NKGB again came to our home. This time – with witnesses from among our own neighbours! – they took Mama! It was just like a nightmare!

Our home had a magnificent veranda with a beautiful wide staircase. I remember it well – how they carried Mama off down this staircase.

My brother and I come out screaming – absolutely screaming in terror. They say they will soon be back to take us to the orphanage.

Exhausted from our screaming; we simply sit on those beautiful steps, crying.

We look up and Mama's here, standing over us!

"They let me go, said it was a mistake."

Thanks be to God that, at least, they corrected that mistake.

* * * * *

So we started little by little to live, or rather to survive. At first no one would give Mama any work. She was the wife of an 'enemy of the people'. Finally, though with difficulty, she was able to find work at a bakery, baking biscuits. But she quit after working there three days. She had to work near the ovens with bare hands, and both hands were scorched. She should have at least received a little training as she wasn't a specialist and burned both hands. "I can't go back there" she said. Then she was able to find work in a cooperative, making locks. At first she did the sorting, then she was a press operator, then a punch operator. Overall, she did well there – and they gave her many bonuses. She was, after all, a woman from a working-class family.

We survived like that till the beginning of the war in 1941. There was no news from our father. Mama still went around the prisons seeking him, and finally they told her that he had been given eight years without the right to correspond, and deported. But people already knew at that time that to be sentenced without the right to correspond meant they were sentenced to execution. If it was simply eight years, that was nothing, but without the right to correspond, it meant the end for him.

We were devastated, and cried a lot for him, but what could we do? We had to live on – life continues. Mama endured it all as best she could. We had to sell everything of value in our house – whatever materials we had, even the shutters from the windows.

Mama had a friend, Aunt Lucy, who would visit every Saturday. She worked at the institute, doing what I don't know, but she would sell whatever we had there, and bring us the money. Thus we were able to survive. It was a good thing that we had been able to buy things when Papa was with us, so that we had them to sell later. Thus we survived until the very beginning of World War II.

Then the war began. At that time, we still hadn't found out anything about Papa. Without being able to correspond, there was nothing he or we could do. It was only recently, that I sent an inquiry, and they sent me a death certificate saying only this:

Anton Vasilovich Voloshin died on the 8th of December 1937 at the age of 39, being shot. Place of burial – unknown.

I tried all the same to find out where he was buried. I sent letters to Ukraine, to Kiev, to Dnipropetrovs'k, everywhere that I could think of, but they all said that it was impossible to know where he was buried. Thus I've never been able to visit my Papa's grave and honour him there.

* * * * *

The war began for us, as for all, suddenly. They told Mama to evacuate, but where could she go with two children? There was no one we could go to, and nowhere to go. Nor was Mama very educated. She could sign her name, as they say, and read a little, being from a hardworking peasant family. She refused to evacuate, saying: "Where could I go? And with whom? I have no relatives, or acquaintances. There's nowhere for me to go."

So we fell under the occupation when the Germans came. They just came, that's all. I had only finished the fifth grade, and the war began. Of course we had to endure many endless difficulties, very many.

244

We were starving, so Mama would barter with anything at all that was left of Papa's things. And then I would go with Mama's friend, Aunt Luba, walking 10 to 12 miles in order to barter his things in surrounding villages. We would barter one of Papa's suits for a little something to eat. We bartered all of my father's things, trying somehow to survive.

Then my brother, four years older than me, began to work as a warehouse worker. He also knew how to drive, as Papa had taught him when he was still alive. There was a monastery forest in the country near us, and when we went there, Papa would often let my brother take the wheel. So he knew how to drive. When Papa was arrested, one of his friends, who managed a garage for ambulances, took my brother to work as a welder. There he studied more and received his drivers licence and was able to begin working. He even worked as a driver for the Germans. He would bring us left-over groceries, and things became a little better as at least we had something to eat.

At last in September our city was due to be liberated. On September 23rd 1943 came our soldiers – Soviets. I began to work in a hospital. I was 15 years old. What else could I do? We had to live. I went to work in a hospital; my brother went to the front. Then I thought that I should find something more permanent. So I went to a military hospital, and they approved me coming to work for them. But I had to get documents from the war commission. I went there and they told me "We can't take you; you're not even 16 years old."

It was already 1944. I returned, asked again, but still they wouldn't take me. Then one time, I showed up and the regular officer was not there, but someone new, who didn't know me. He said: "Documents". I said: "I don't have any documents, they were all lost." And I was a strapping young girl, well built and not too skinny. Since I was already with this hospital, they took me. The hospital was reassigned to the front line and I remained with them till the end of the war.

By then I had reached the city of Dresden in Germany. The hospital stood outside Dresden, in the city of Shpremberg, on the Shpree River. The end of the war found me there. They had already announced Germany's surrender and we knew on April 30th that we had won.

All occupied territory was being surrounded by the Soviets; first Ukraine, then Belarus was caught in the ring. Already the banners were being raised over the Reichstag. By May 5th we were all crying "Victory!" What joy it was indeed! Everyone left the hospital, except the wounded. The relief was universal. There was a ceasefire on the 8th, and victory was declared on May 9th.

After Dresden, after the proclamation of the end of the war, the hospital moved to Austria, to the city of Shtyreray. This is somewhere close to Vienna. We were accommodated in a monastery, living in the cells like monks. Many wounded were still arriving, even though victory was proclaimed. They came out of the trenches to try and get on our side. I remained there until the end of November 1945. There I was demobilised, and returned home.

* * * * *

I returned home, but there was no home, only starvation. There was so much starvation in Dnipropetrovs'k after the war! I would go out in the evening and everything would seem normal; but go out in the morning and already people were lying dead and decaying; corpses laying everywhere, and trucks coming to gather them up. One had to have seen it and experienced it to believe this terrible hunger at the end of the war.

Mama lived in a private apartment and was also starving. Even her legs were swelling. My brother was demobilised in western Ukraine, where he had been a tank driver. He stayed on in the city of Kovel and brought Mama there.

But I was recruited to come with the young communist league here to the north. My hometown ceased to be my home, as no one and nothing of ours remained there – only the past memories of my childhood, both happy and unhappy.

I came to Magadan in 1953, and brought Mama here in 1964. I worked on an outlying communal farm for 32 years. There I married and had two children. I divorced my husband as he was such a heavy drinker, not wanting to work, and loving to drink. I wasn't very lucky in love, so rather than suffer, better to live alone. My son was one year old.

I brought my mother here, and thus we lived. I worked with the animals on a farm. I often came home completely tired from work; no good to do anything else. It often happened that I worked 24 hours at a time. If

246

someone didn't show up, I'd work their shift, go home for 12 hours and report back for my shift. It was good that Mama was there to fix something to eat. I'd come home, eat, sleep and again go back to work.

That was life.

* * * * *

Now when we old-timers get together, I am honoured everywhere, as there are fewer and fewer left of us. Who will be left by next year? I have received my medals: the Order of the Great Patriotic War "for victory over Germany", the Zhukova medal and anniversary mementos. How very many of us are already gone! I look at photos, and think: "This one is already gone, and that one also."

My photos are in a book about Magadan, and on display in the City Hall. I visit the schools, meet with the children and tell them about the war. I go to the meetings of the repressed. I think that someone who has lived a life such as mine needs to do all of this. We're getting older, but as long as we are still alive, we need to do this – if only for the sake of fellowship between ourselves.

I've met new people at these meetings. Walking throughout the city, I've had people greet me, and I them. It's pleasant to meet people in such a way. We definitely need community, especially at our age.

The certificate of rehabilitation for Anton Vacilevich Voloshin states:

'Place of work – driver for the city communal farm. Condemned on November 25th 1937 by the NKGB of the USSR and procurator of the USSR to death before the firing squad. Method of punishment: shooting. Arrested 23rd August 1937. Decision to carry out punishment reached 8th December 1937.
Based on the first article of law of Ukraine about the rehabilitation of victims of political repression in Ukraine of April 17th 1991, Anton Vasilevich Voloshin was rehabilitated on the February 6th 2002 by the army procurator of Ukraine, northern region. Evgenia Antonovna Voloshin was left underage without the support of a father, unjustly repressed for political motives, and rehabilitated.'

Glossary of Terms

Article 58 – A notorious article of the Soviet Penal Code used to arrest those suspected of counter-revolutionary activities. Its broad scope empowered the secret police to arrest and imprison anyone deemed to be suspicious

Balalaika – A Russian string instrument with a triangular body and three, or sometimes six, strings

Banderovets – a bandit or partisan supporter of separatist movements

Beria, Lavrentiy Pavlovich (1899-1953) – Head of the NKVD and thus chief of the Soviet security and police service. Viewed as the executor of Stalin's Great Purge of the 1930s. Executed on the orders of Nikita Khrushchev in 1953

Berlag – The labour camp system established in the Magadan region by Lavrentiy Beria (*see* **Beria**, *above)*

Borscht – A vegetable soup from eastern Europe and Russia, usually made with beetroot

Burki – Padded cloth boots

Chaika – A grocery store. The name means seagull

Dacha – A small house, often just a shed or hut, in the country usually with a garden.

Domra – A long-necked Russian string instrument with three or four steel strings; often used to play the lead melody in balalaika ensembles

Gulag – Acronym of *Glavnoye Upravleniye Ispravitelno-trudovykh Lagerey i kolonii*. This was the USSR government department which administered labour camps. The term came to be used for the camps themselves

Invalidka – The home or hospital for the very sick and invalids

Kasha – A form of wheat porridge that has been eaten in Eastern European cuisine for more than 1,000 years

KGB – *Komitet Gosudarstvennoĭ Bezopasnosti*. Russian Committee of State Security, the USSR's state security police responsible for external espionage, internal counter-intelligence and internal crimes against the state

Kiosk – A small booth with groceries

Kolyma – A river flowing north from near Magadan, giving its name to the entire region

Kopeck – Penny, one one-hundredth of a rouble, the Russian unit of currency

KpCh – Communist Party of China

KVZhD – The Chinese Eastern (or Far East) Railway in north-eastern China. Abbreviation from the Russian name *Kitaysko-Vostochnaya Zheleznaya Doroga*

Nagayevo Bay – The bay on which Magadan sits, all prisoners to the Kolyma were brought here

NKVD – *Narodny Komissariat Vnutrennikh Del*. Russian state security department, forerunner of the KGB. It ran the Gulag system of forced labour

Oblast – Russian political administrative region, like a state

Pani – Russian for 'Grandma'

Parasha – A large chamber pot

Pea-coat – A padded sailor's jacket

Perestroika – Economic reforms introduced in the USSR by President Mikhail Gorbachev in June 1985

Rouble – Russian unit of currency

Sateen – A cotton fabric with a satin-like finish, often found in bed sheets

Seksot – An informer

Siberia – All the large interior portion of Russia, East of the Urals. Technically Magadan isn't in Siberia, but even east of Siberia

Sotok – A unit of measurement for land

Stalin, Joseph (1879-1953) – General Secretary of the Communist Party of Russia from 1922 to 1953. Stalin's influence within the party saw him take dictatorial control of the Soviet Union. His 1930s programs of industrialisation and collectivisation, coupled with a regime of political oppression, cost some 20 million lives

Stevedore – A person employed at a dock to load and unload ships

Swede – A green weed

Taiga – A forest of Russia

Trassa – The highway, the road heading from Magadan north to the mines and camps

Troika – A court of three judges

Yzvar – A dried fruit compote, often used to sweeten hot drinks such as tea

Zemlianka – A form of bunker consisting of a hole dug in the ground with a roof over it

Złoty – Polish unit of currency

Zone – The fenced off area of a camp, with guards walking the perimeter

Aid to the Church in Need

Aid to the Church in Need supports the faithful wherever they are persecuted, oppressed or in pastoral need. ACN is a Catholic charity, helping to bring Christ to the world.

ACN was founded in Christmas Day 1947 by Father Werenfried van Straaten and is now a universal pastoral charity of the Catholic Church, with thousands of projects all over the world:

- Seminarians are trained
- Bibles and religious literature are printed
- Priests and religious are supported
- Refugees are helped
- Churches and chapels are built and restored
- Over 43 million of ACN's Child's Bibles have been printed in more than 150 languages
- Religious programmes are broadcast

For regular updates from the suffering Church around the world, and to view our full range of books, cards, gifts and music, please log on to **www.acnuk.org**

Aid to the Church in Need

In the UK
12-14 Benhill Avenue   Tel: 020 8642 8668
Sutton   Email: acn@acnuk.org
SM1 4DA   www.acnuk.org

In Australia
PO Box 6245   Tel: +61 (0) 2 9679 1929
Blacktown DC   Email: info@aidtochurch.org
NSW 2148   www.aidtochurch.org

In Canada
PO Box 670, STN H   Tel: +1 (1) 800 585 6333
Montreal   Email: info@acn-aed-ca.org
QC H3G 2M6   www.acn-aed-ca.org

In Ireland
151 St Mobhi Road   Tel: +353 (0) 1 83 77 516
Glasnevin   Email: churchinneed@eircom.net
Dublin 9   www.acnirl.org

In the USA
725 Leonard Street   Tel: +1 (1) 800 628 6333
PO Box 220384   Email: info@acnusa.org
Brooklyn   www.churchinneed.com
NY 11222-0384